Copyright: Patty Duffy
All Rights Reserved
No part of this book can be copied or sold
without prior written permission from author.
ISBN: 9798533367592

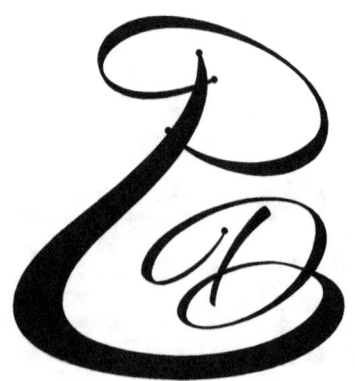

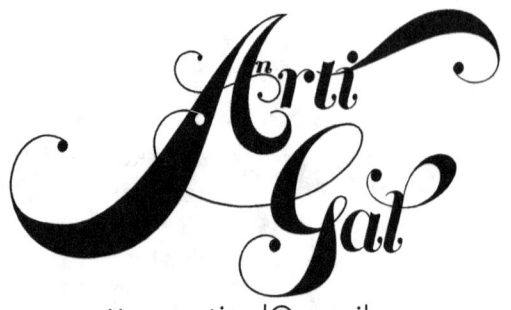

patty.anartigal@gmail.com

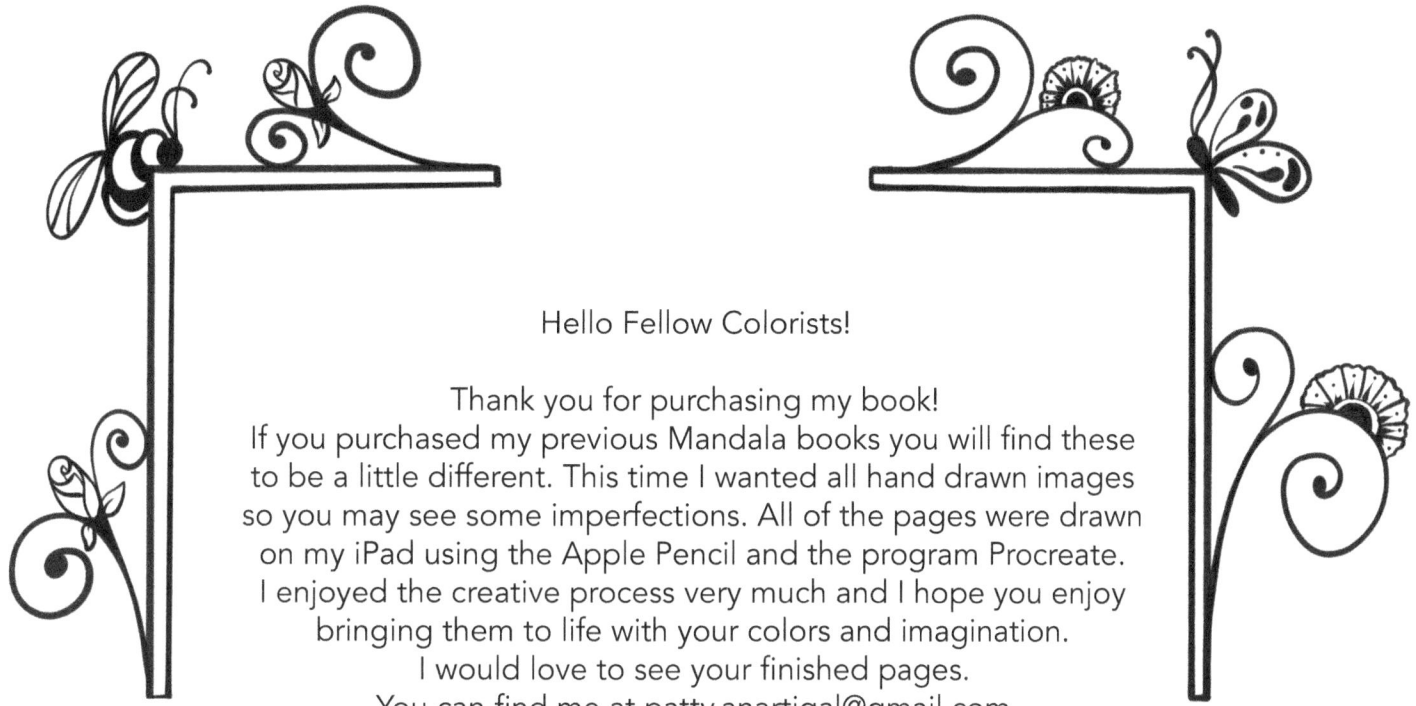

Hello Fellow Colorists!

Thank you for purchasing my book!
If you purchased my previous Mandala books you will find these
to be a little different. This time I wanted all hand drawn images
so you may see some imperfections. All of the pages were drawn
on my iPad using the Apple Pencil and the program Procreate.
I enjoyed the creative process very much and I hope you enjoy
bringing them to life with your colors and imagination.
I would love to see your finished pages.
You can find me at patty.anartigal@gmail.com

I've included an area at the bottom of each page giving you the
space to swatch your colors as you go. Often times I will start
a page only to get interrupted and then have to guess which
pencils or markers I used, now I can see at a glance and can
easily pick up where I left off.

Mandalas are meant to be relaxing and fun.
There are no mistakes, but if you feel like you made one,
make the same mistake all the way around
and it will blend in beautifully.

You can use pens, pencils, colored pencils, gel pens,
markers or what ever you have on hand.
Please test markers as they may bleed through to next page.
You can place a piece of paper behind your coloring page to help
prevent markers bleeding through.

Thank you and have fun!
Happy Coloring!

Patty

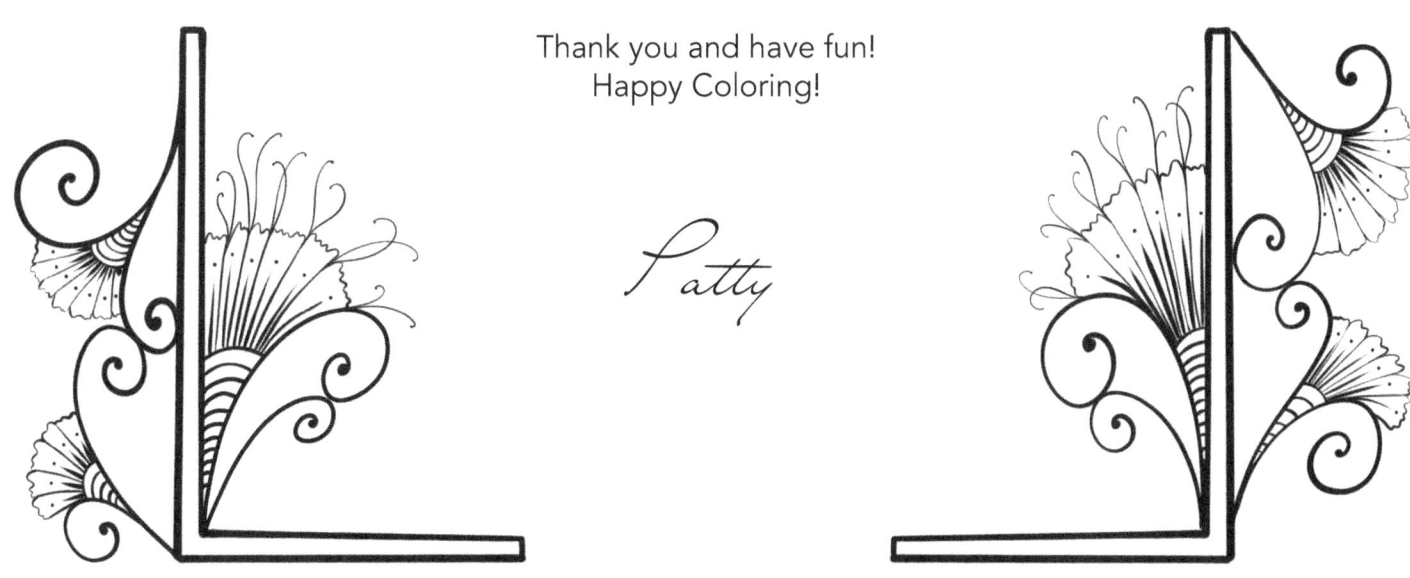

This Book Belongs To:
_____
_____
_____
_____
_____

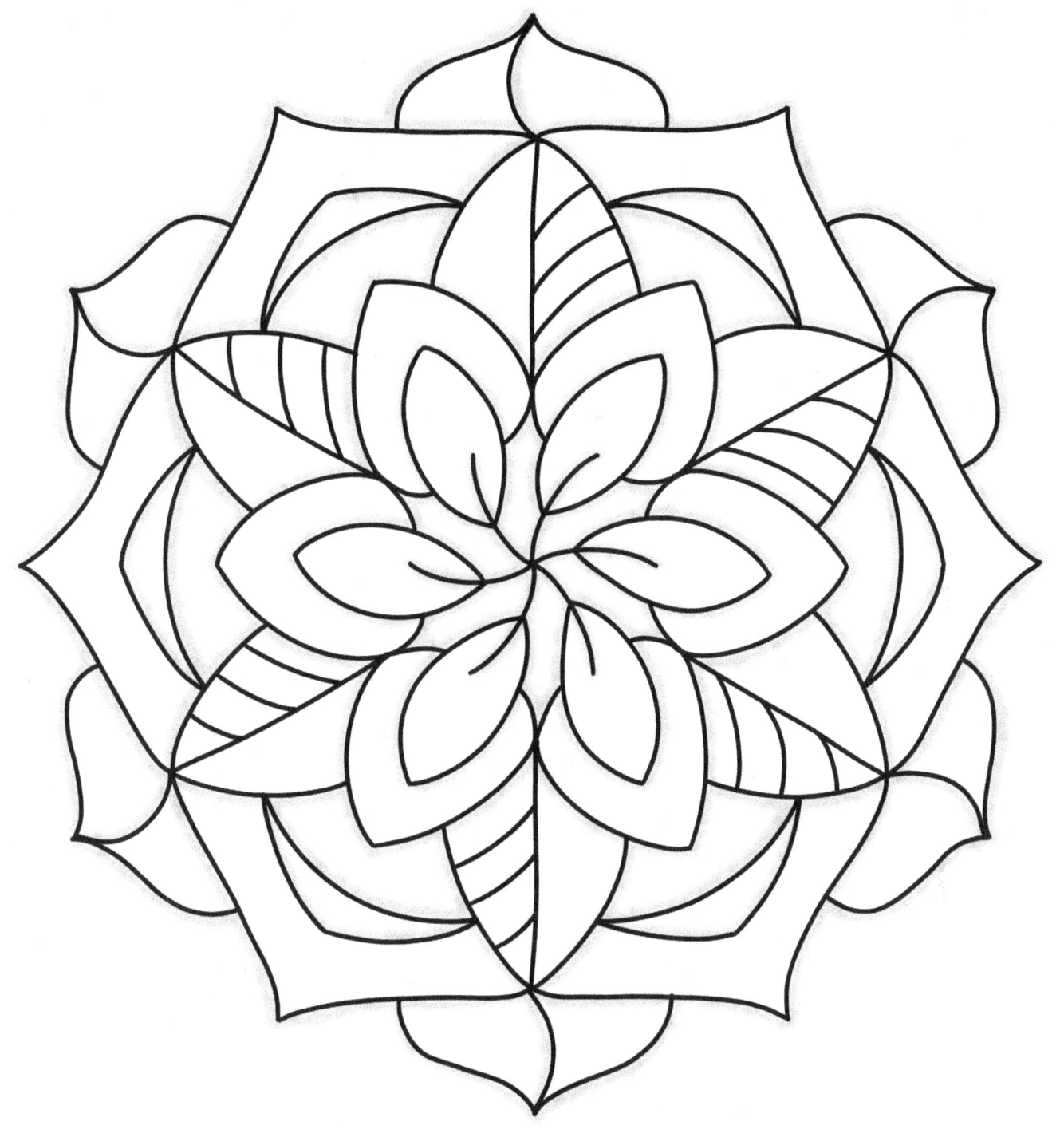

Date:_____ Colorist:_____
Media Type: _____
Media Test Area:

Date:_____ Colorist: _____
Media Type: _____
Media Test Area:

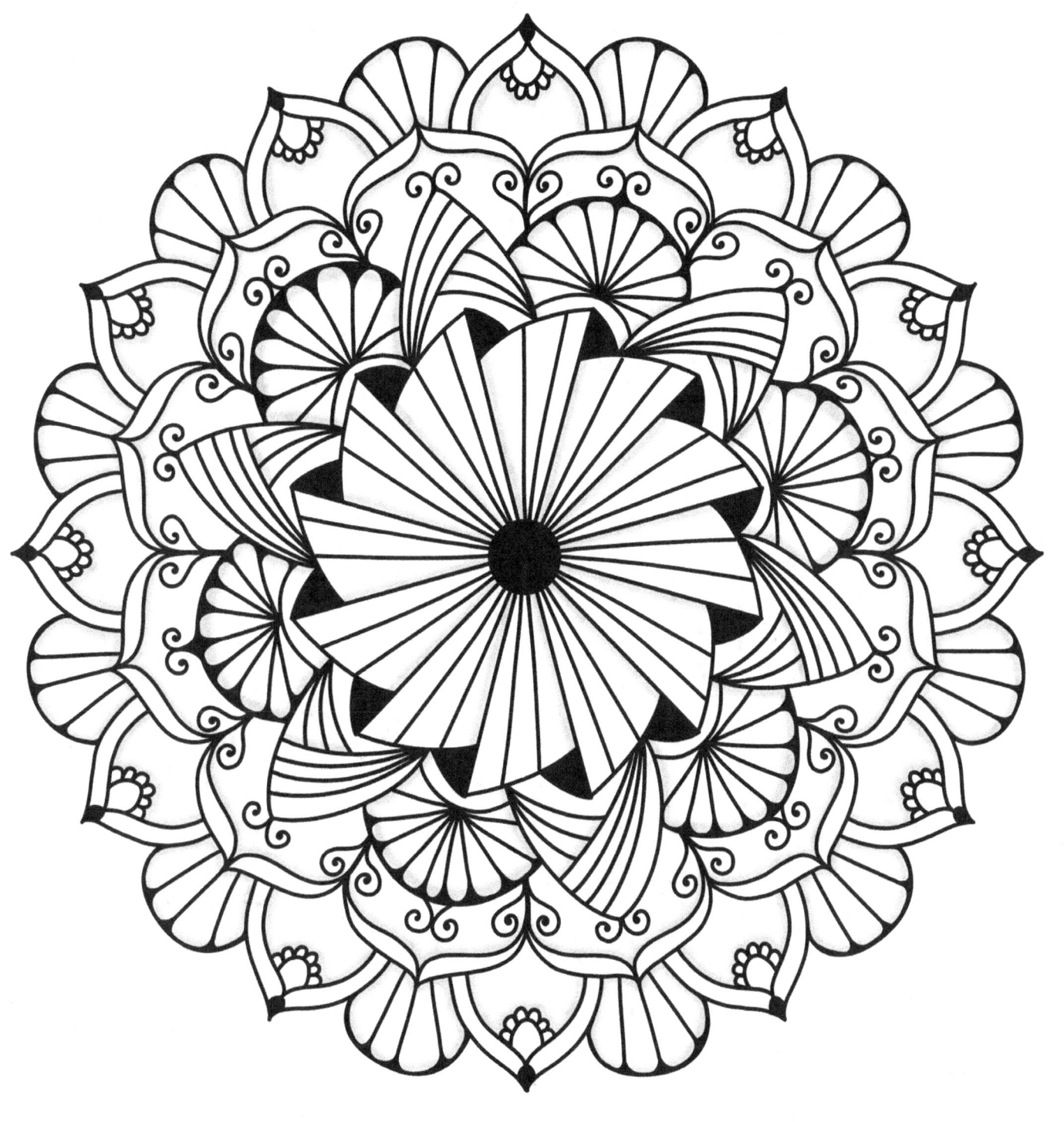

Date:_____   Colorist:_____
Media Type: _____
Media Test Area:

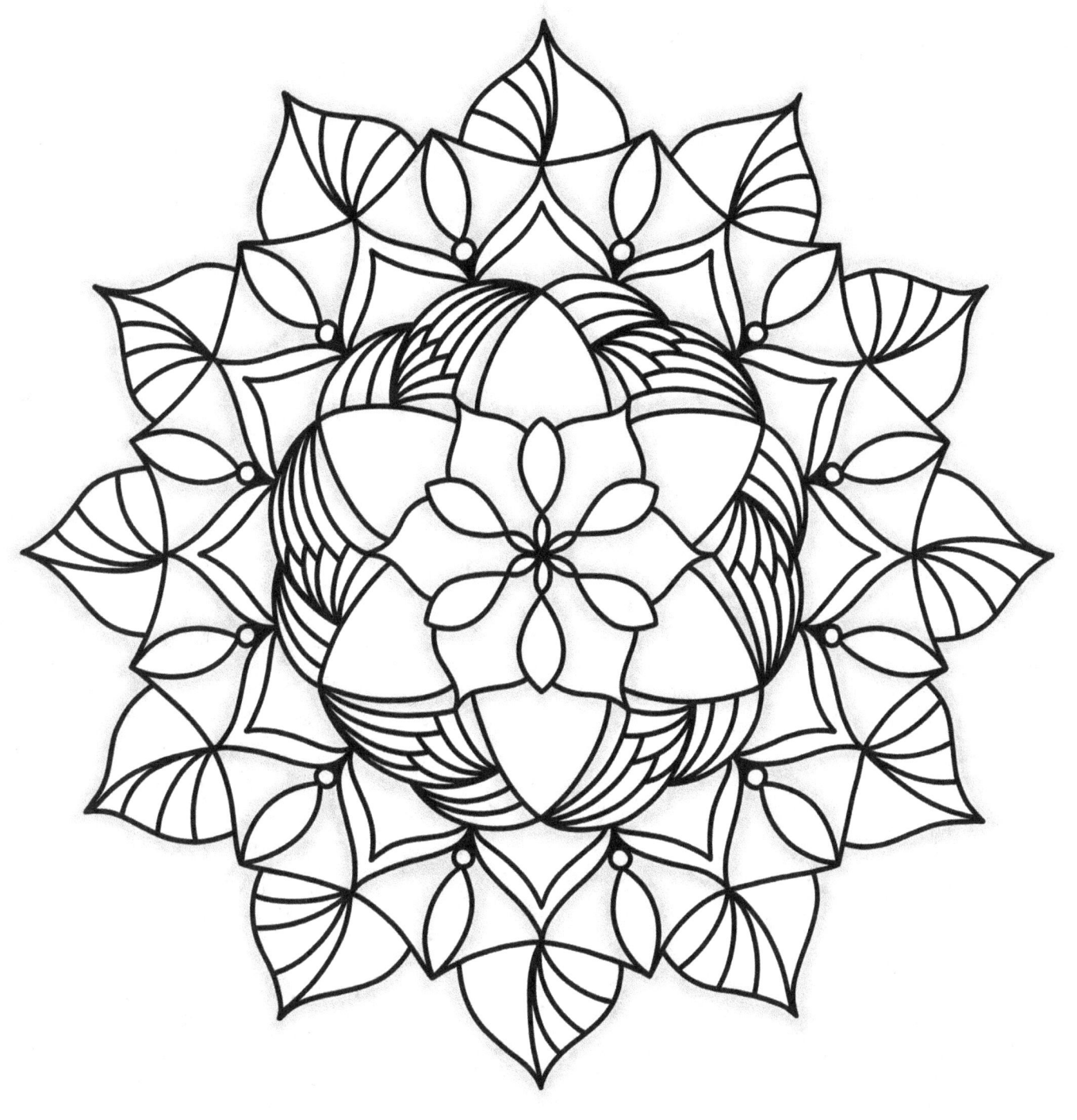

Date:_____ Colorist: _____
Media Type: _____
Media Test Area:

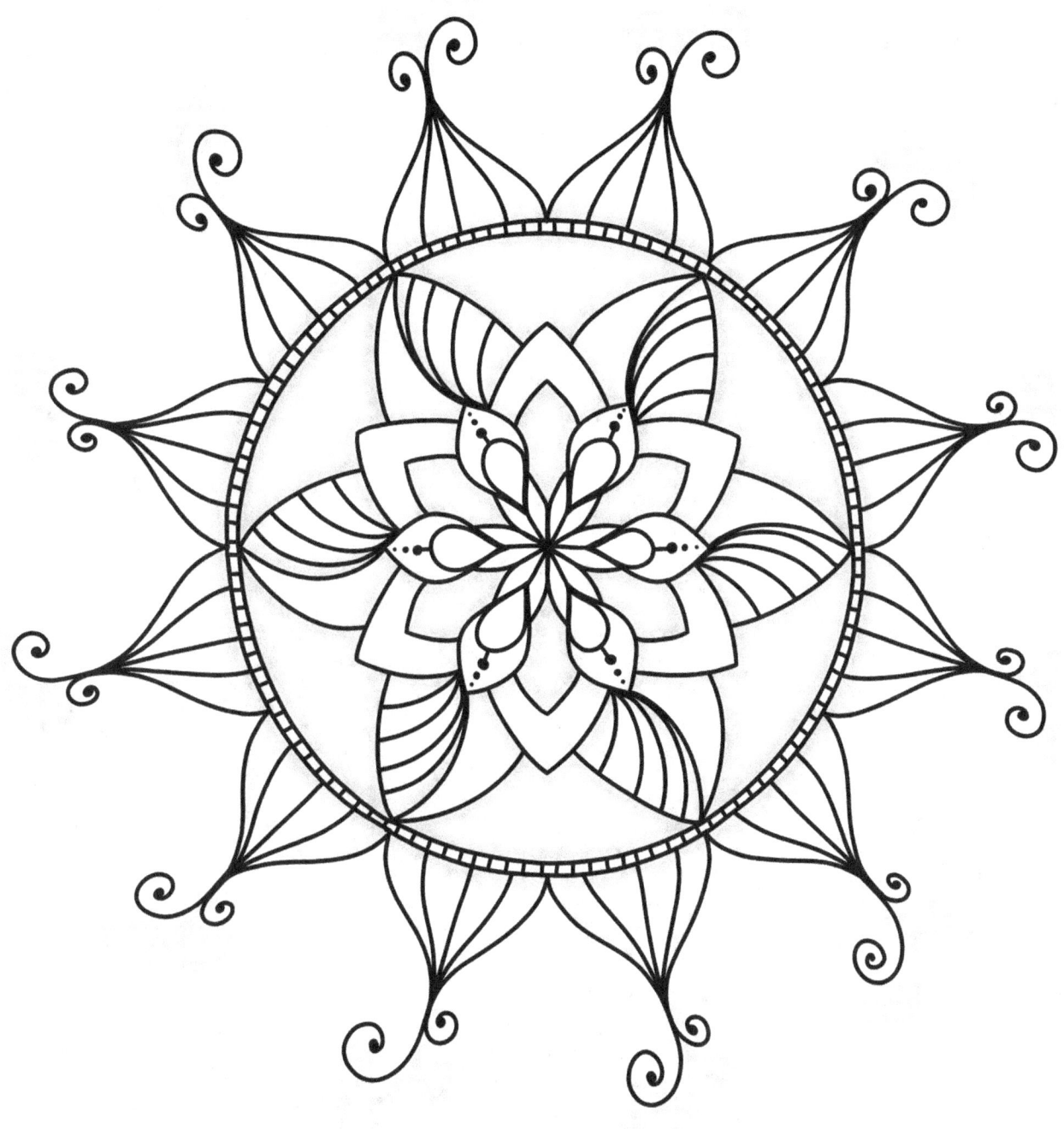

Date:_____   Colorist: _____
Media Type: _____
Media Test Area:

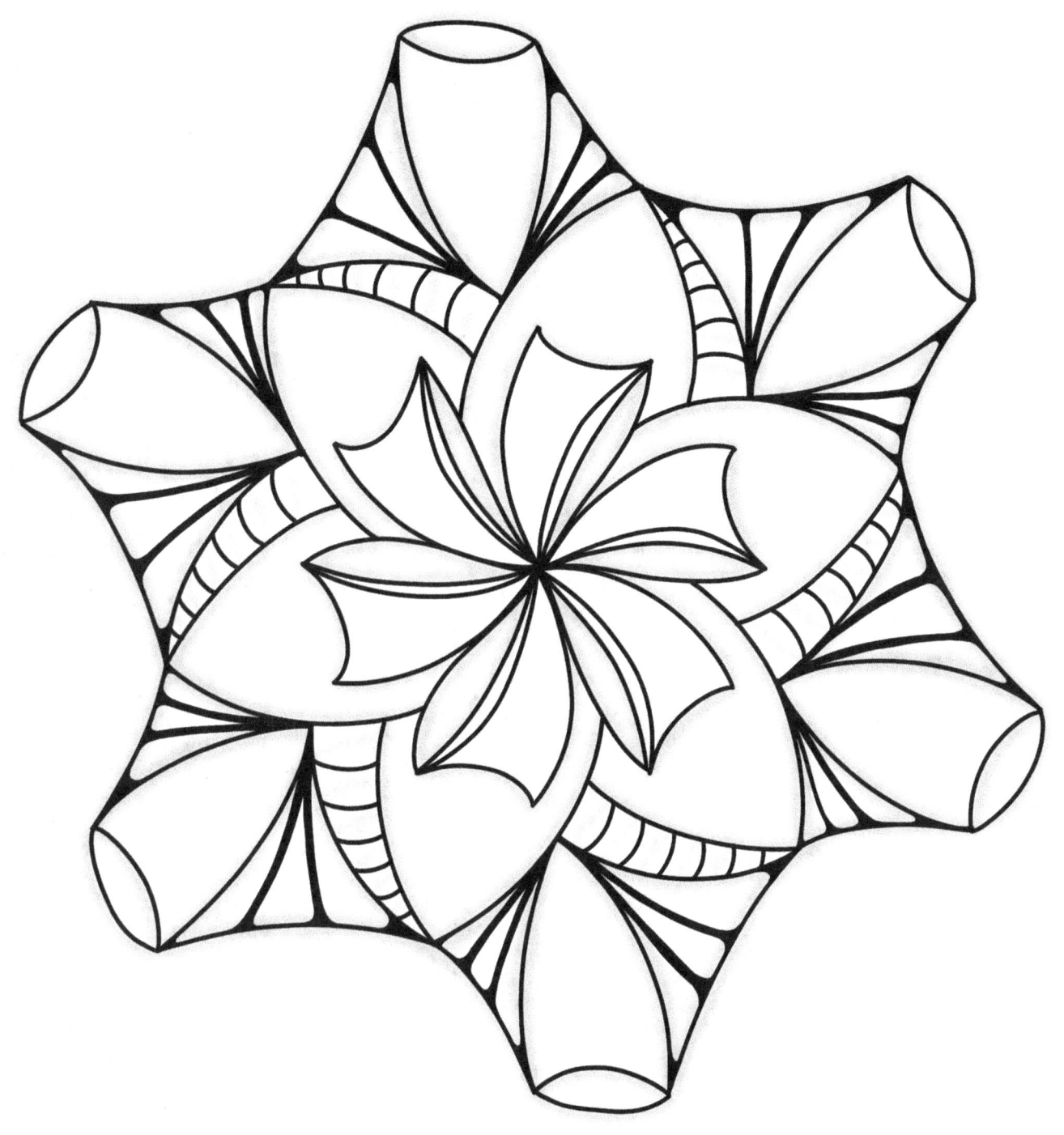

Date:_____ Colorist: _____
Media Type: _____
Media Test Area:

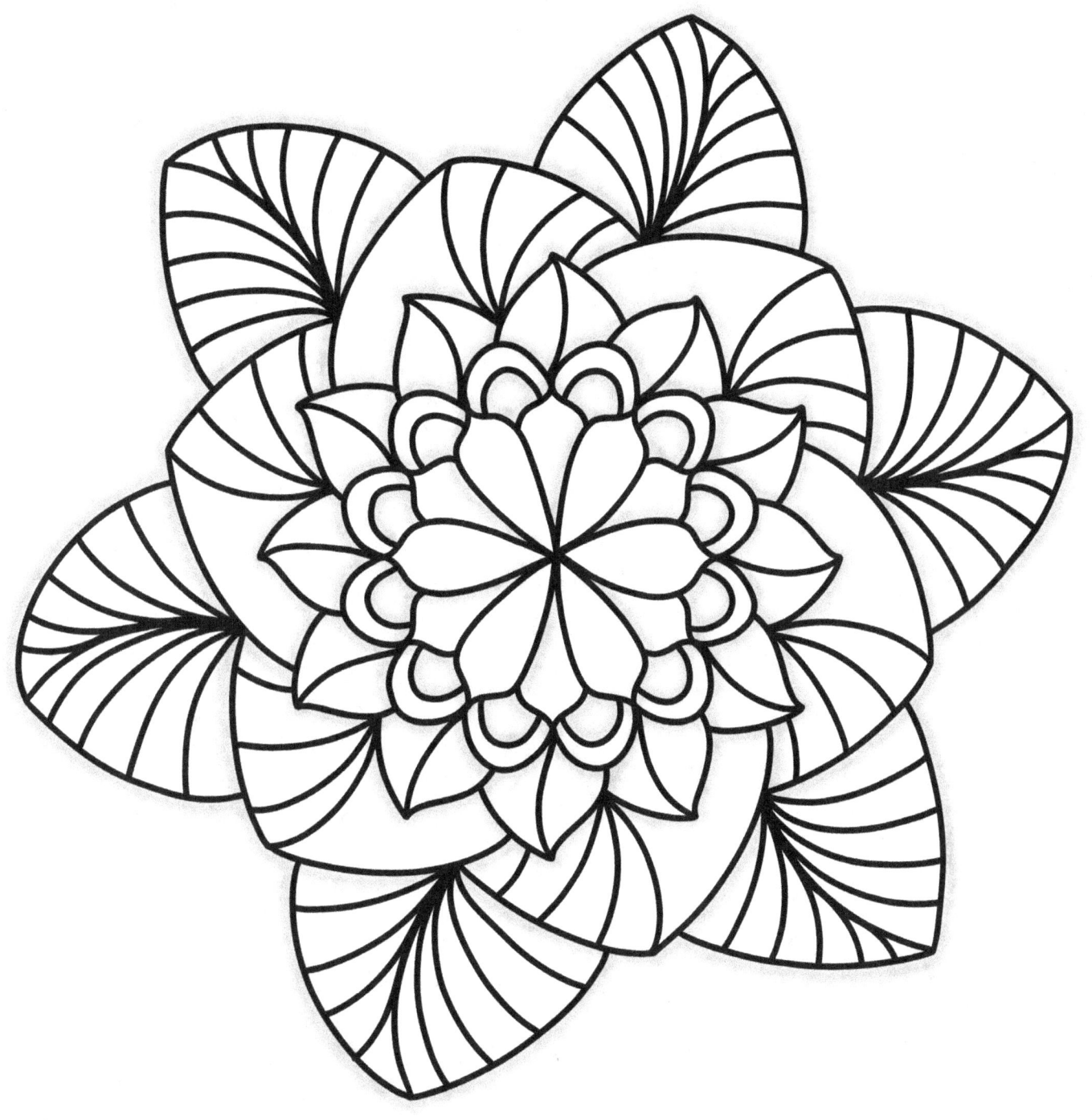

Date:_____ Colorist:_____
Media Type: _____
Media Test Area:

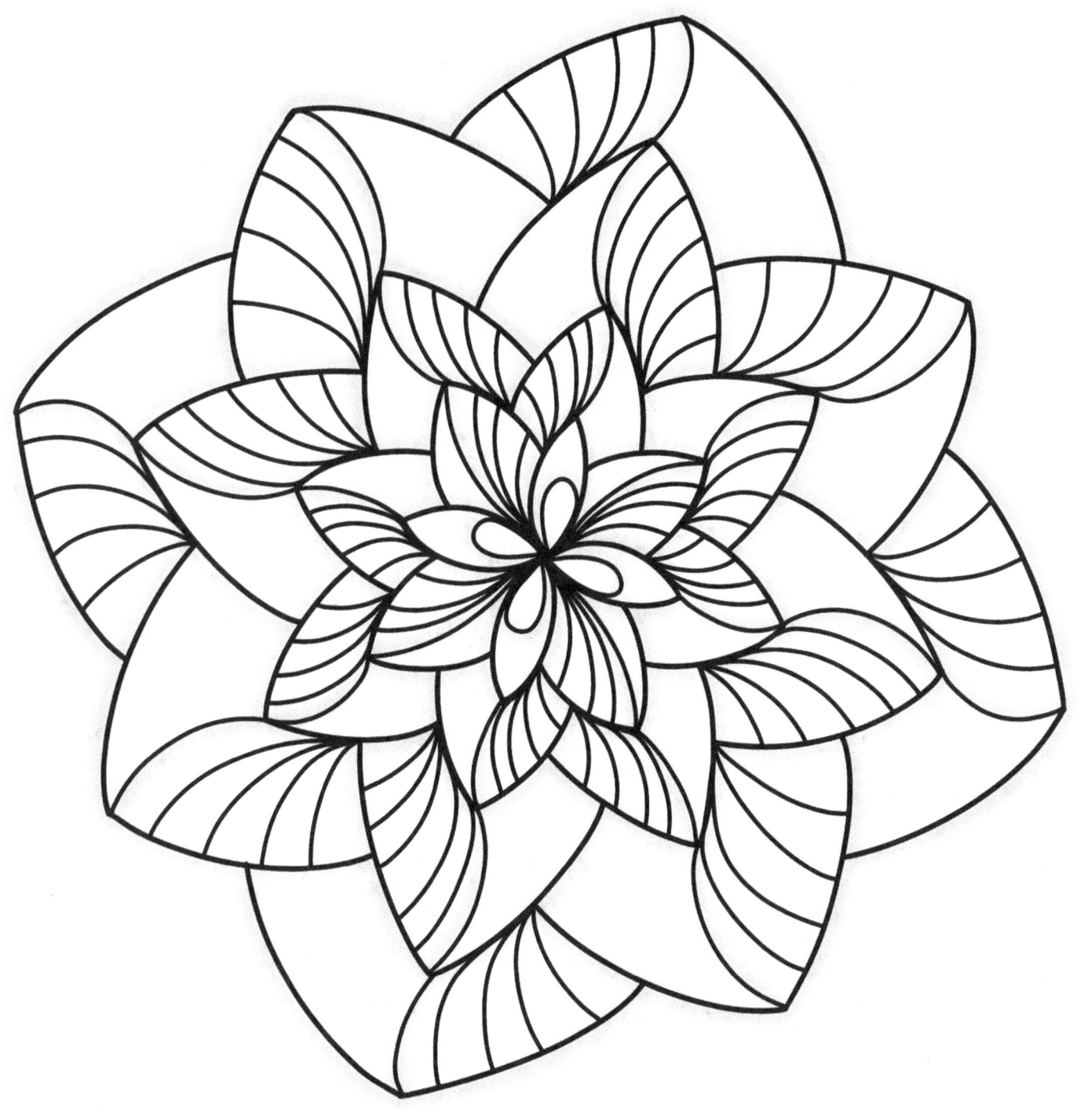

Date:_____   Colorist: _____
Media Type: _____
Media Test Area:

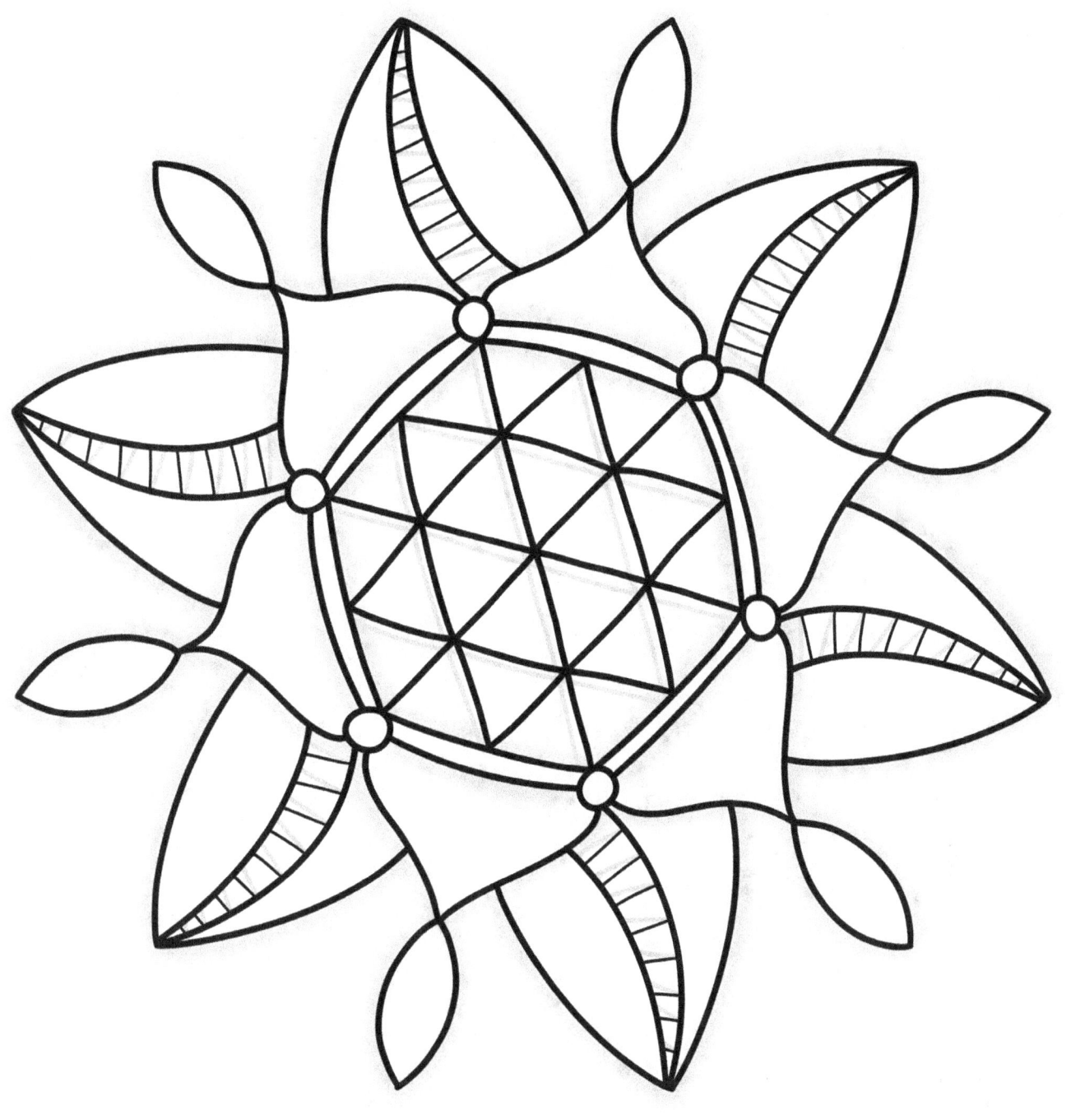

Date:_____ Colorist: _____
Media Type: _____
Media Test Area:

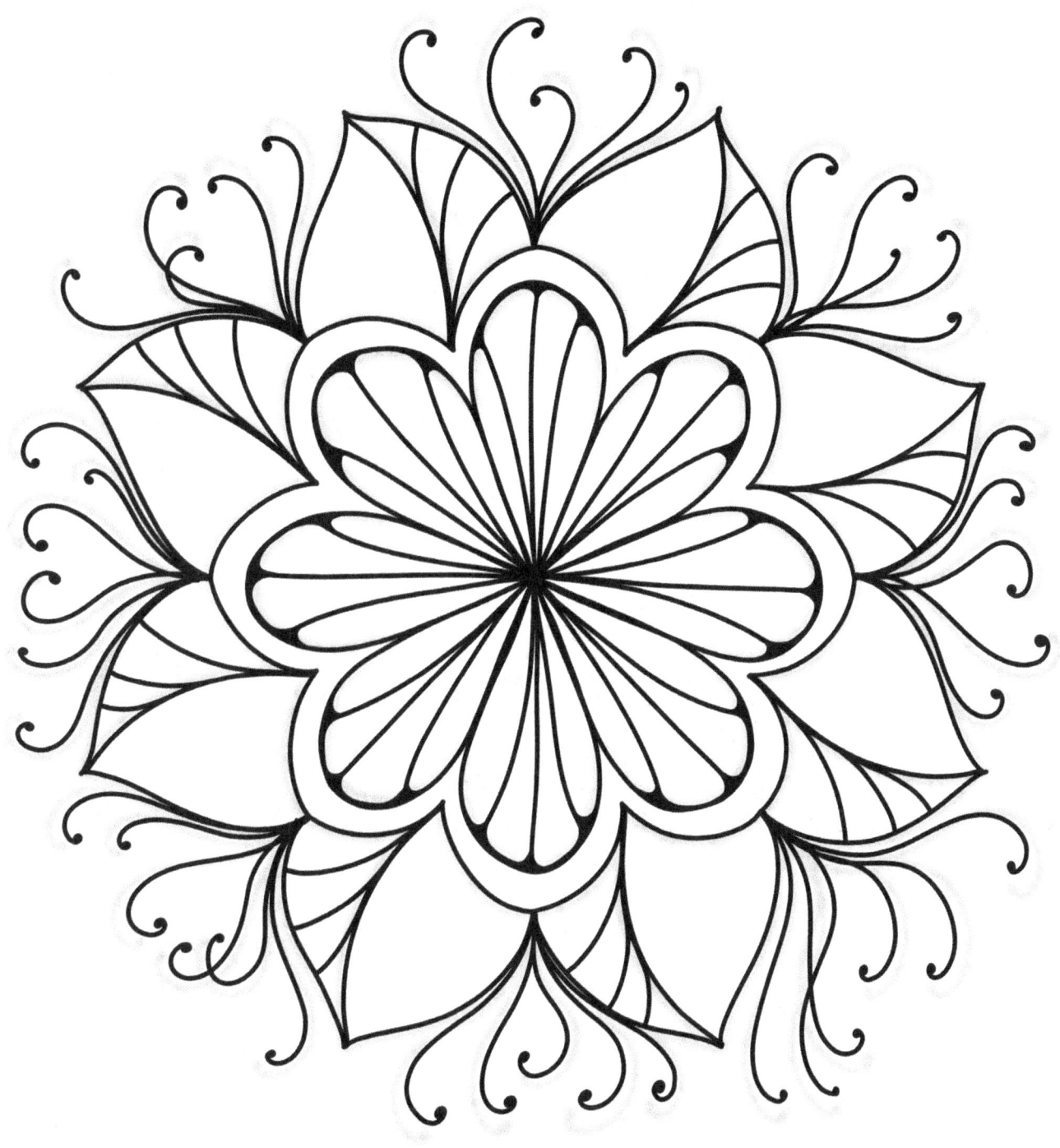

Date:_____ Colorist: _____
Media Type: _____
Media Test Area:

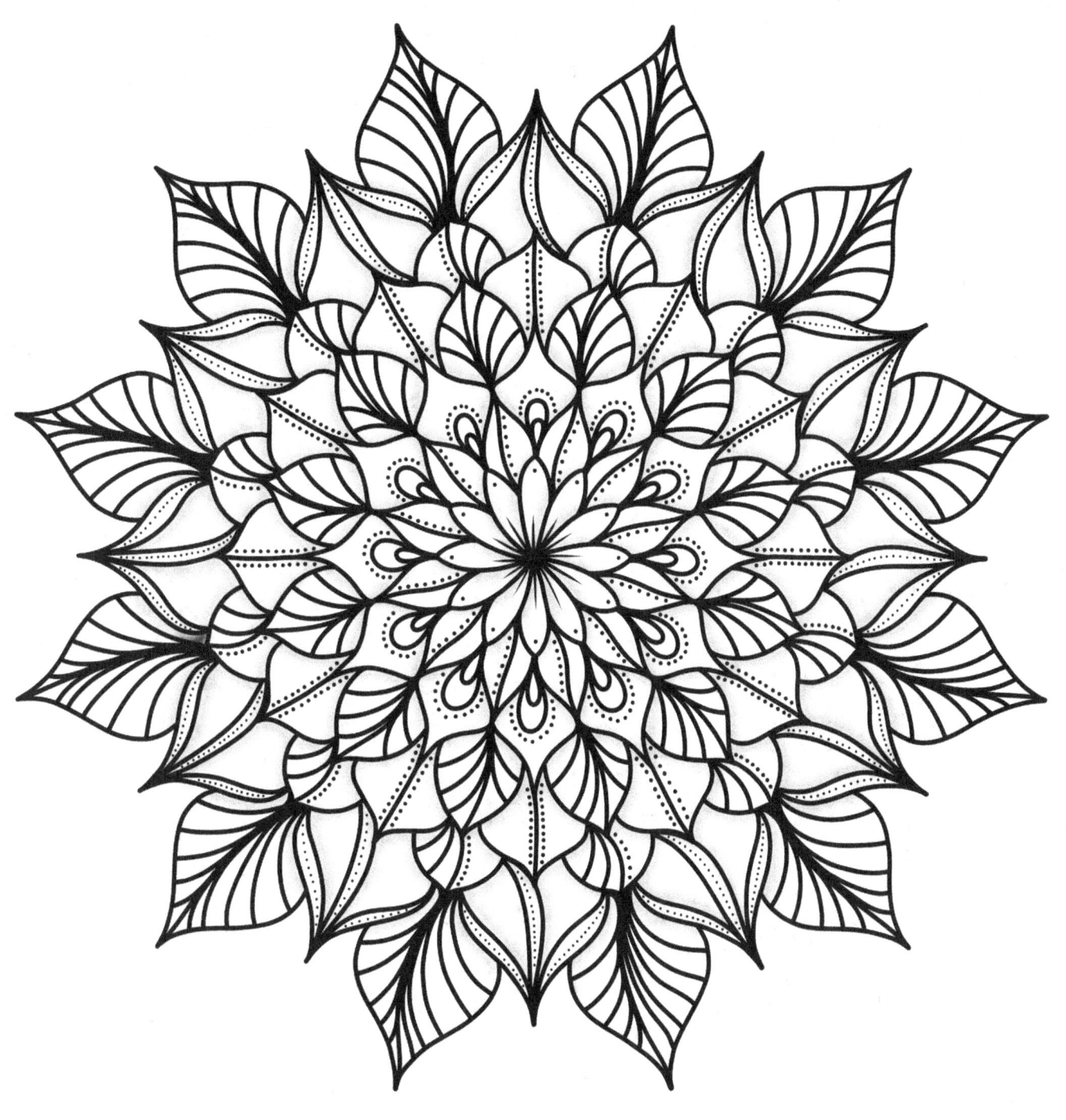

Date:_____   Colorist: _____
Media Type: _____
Media Test Area:

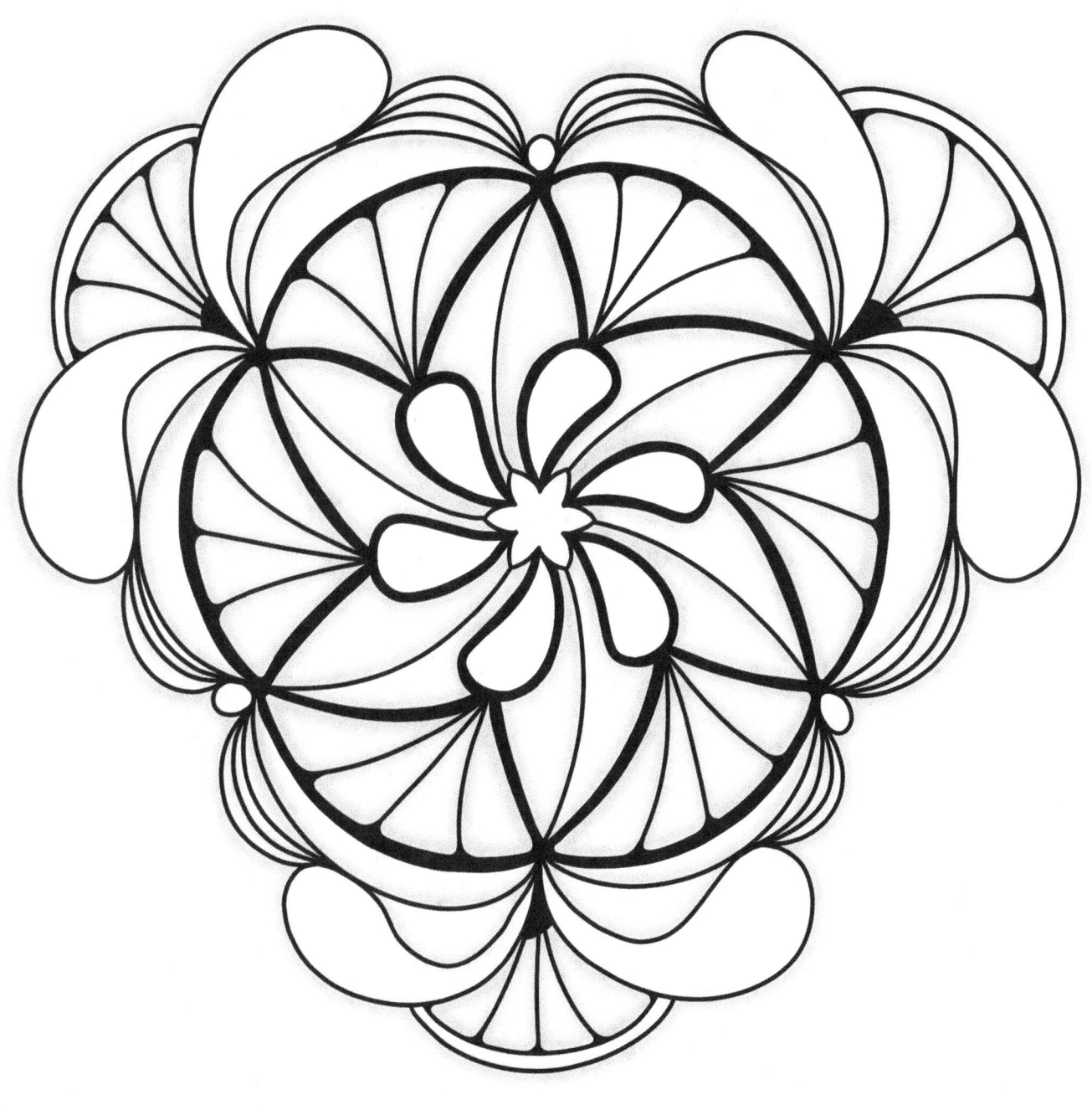

Date:_____ Colorist: _____
Media Type: _____
Media Test Area:

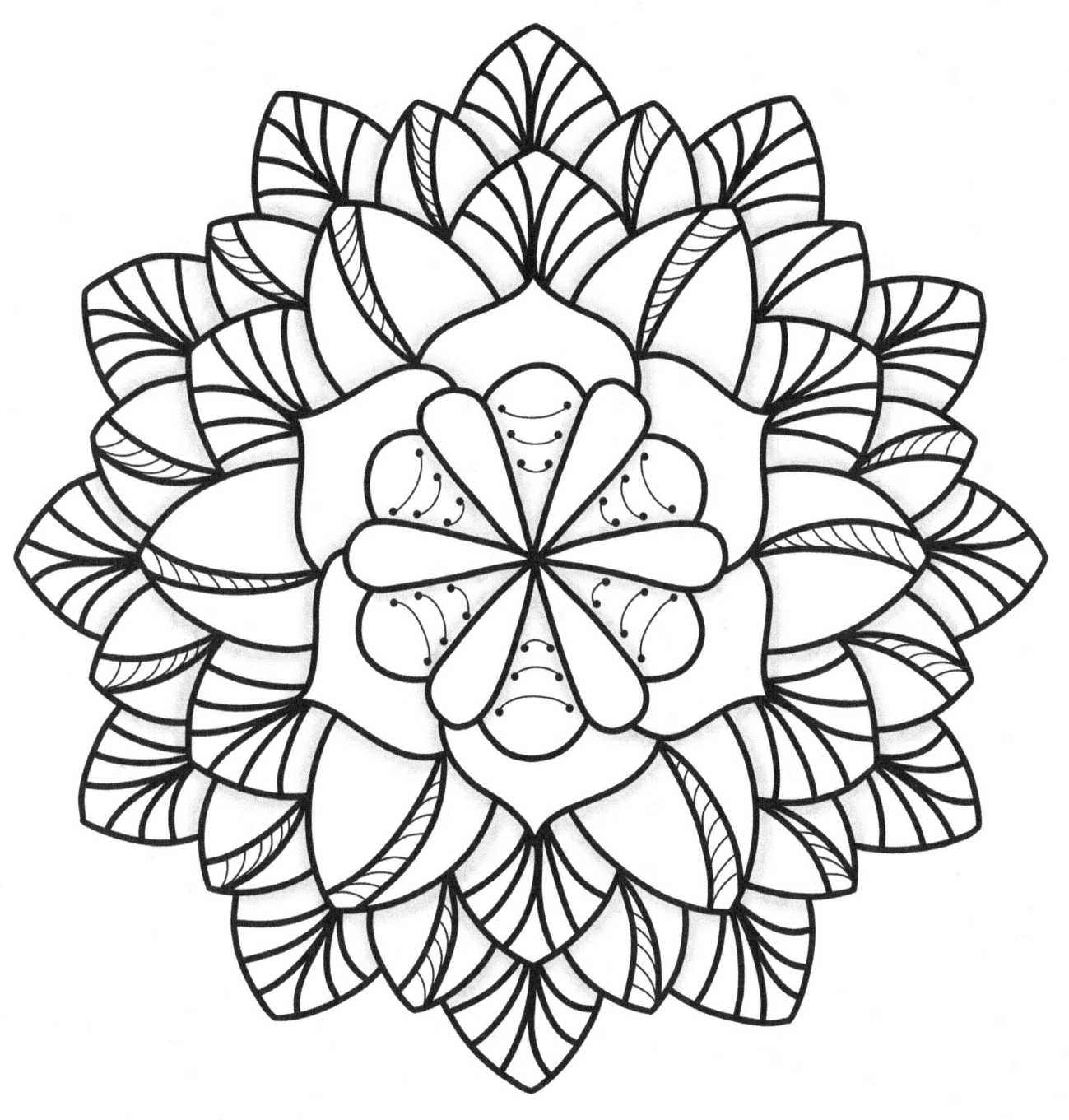

Date:_____   Colorist: _____
Media Type: _____
Media Test Area:

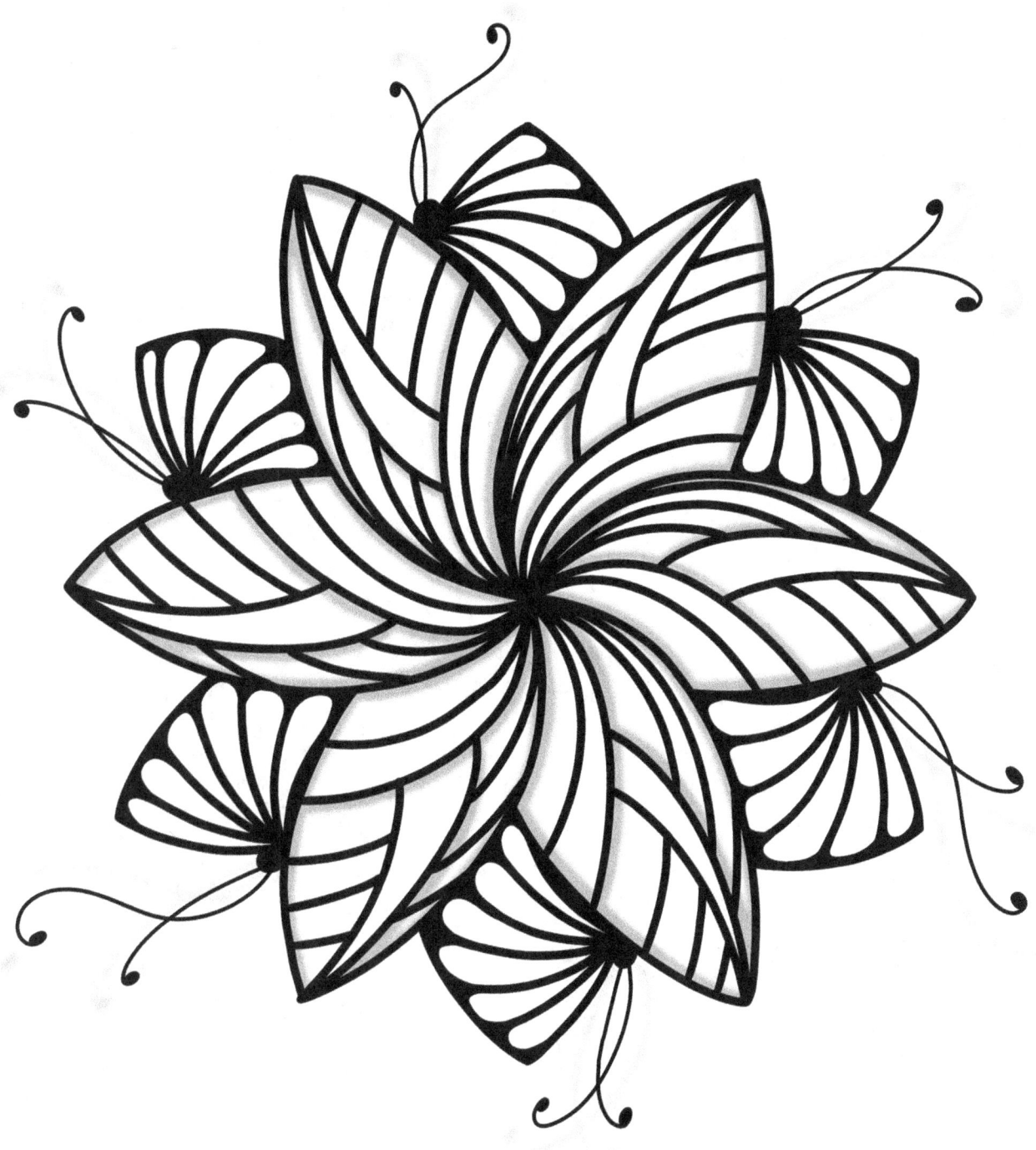

Date:_____ Colorist: _____
Media Type: _____
Media Test Area:

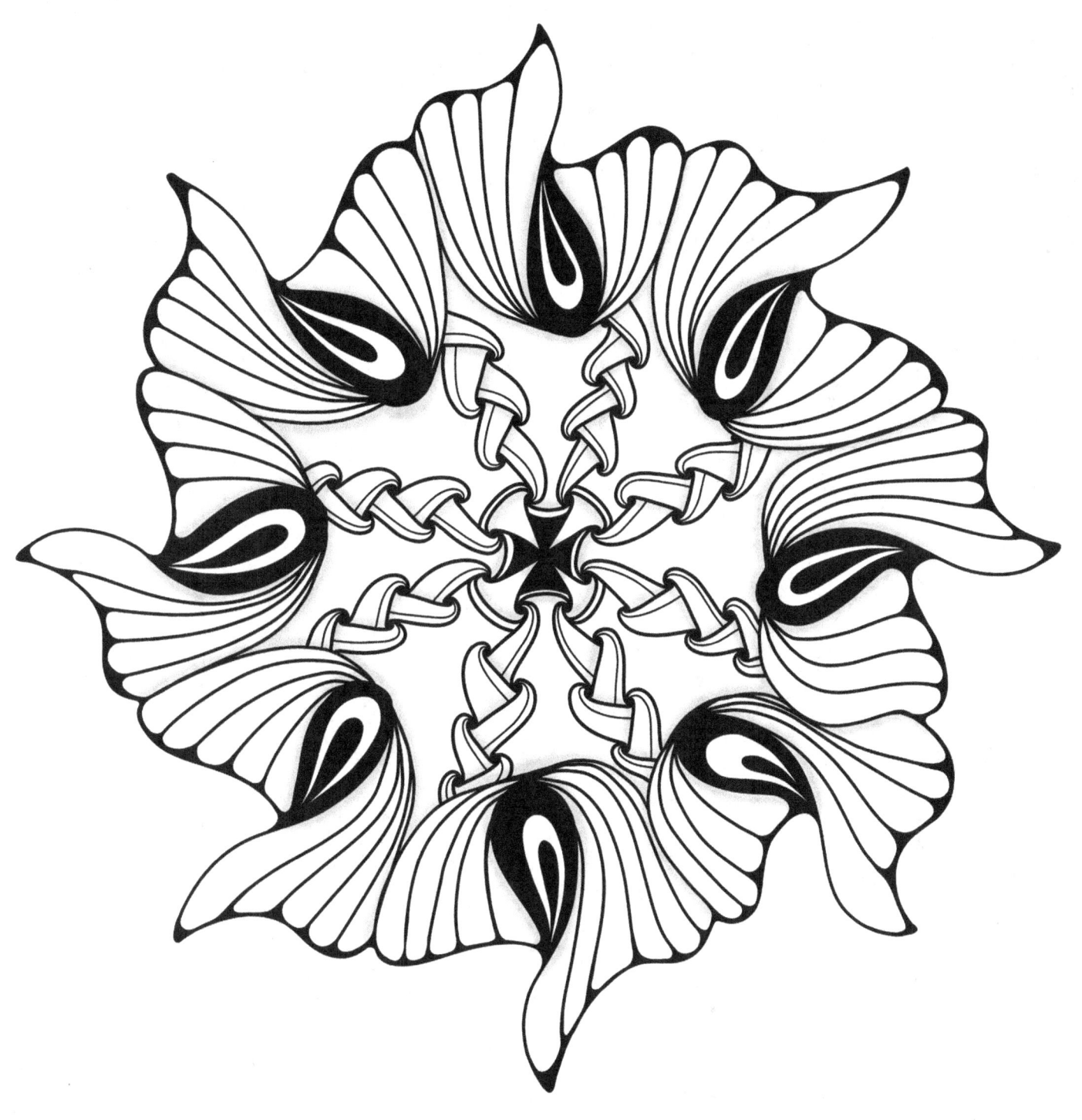

Date:_____ Colorist:_____
Media Type: _____
Media Test Area:

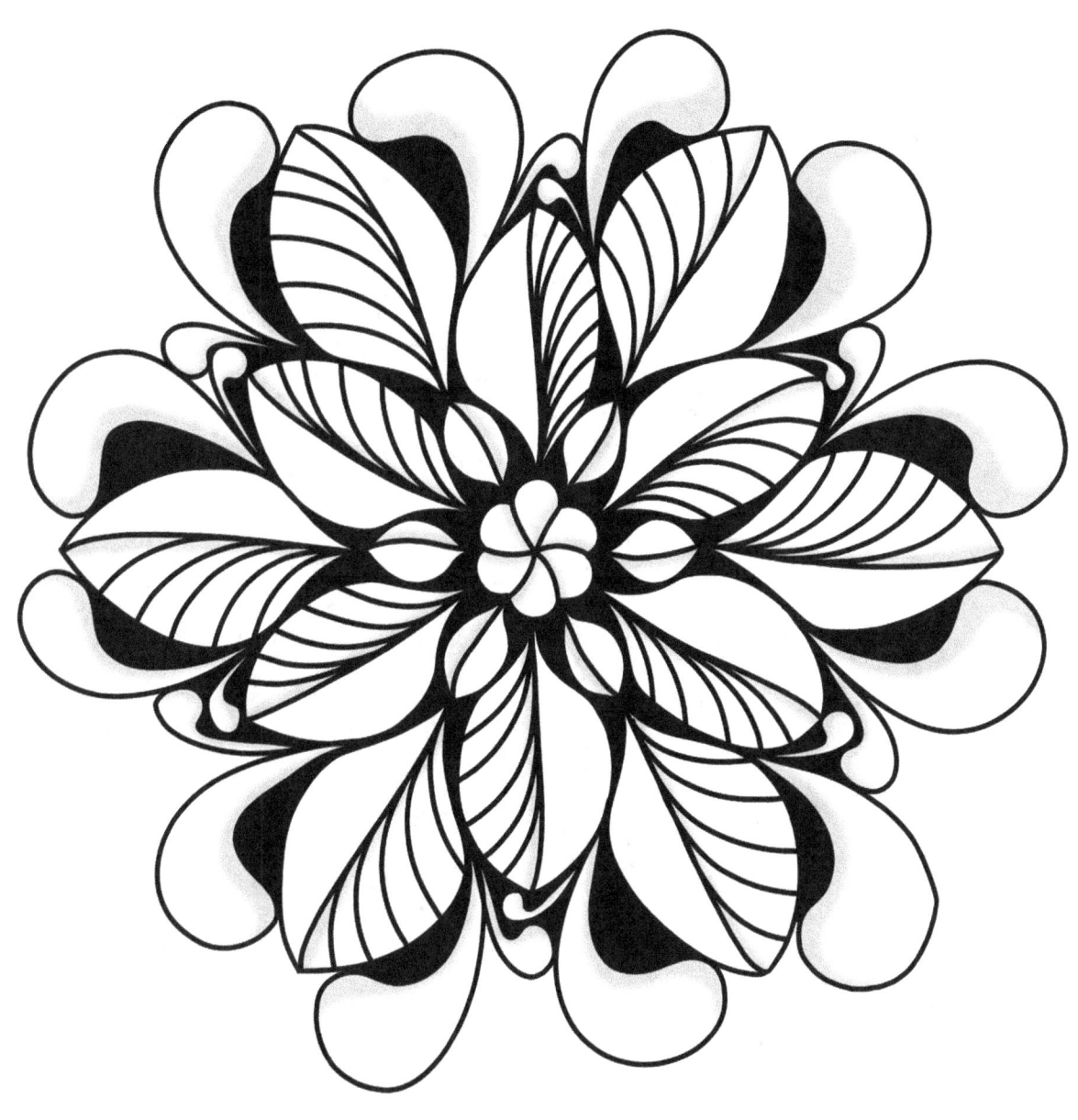

Date:_____ Colorist: _____
Media Type: _____
Media Test Area:

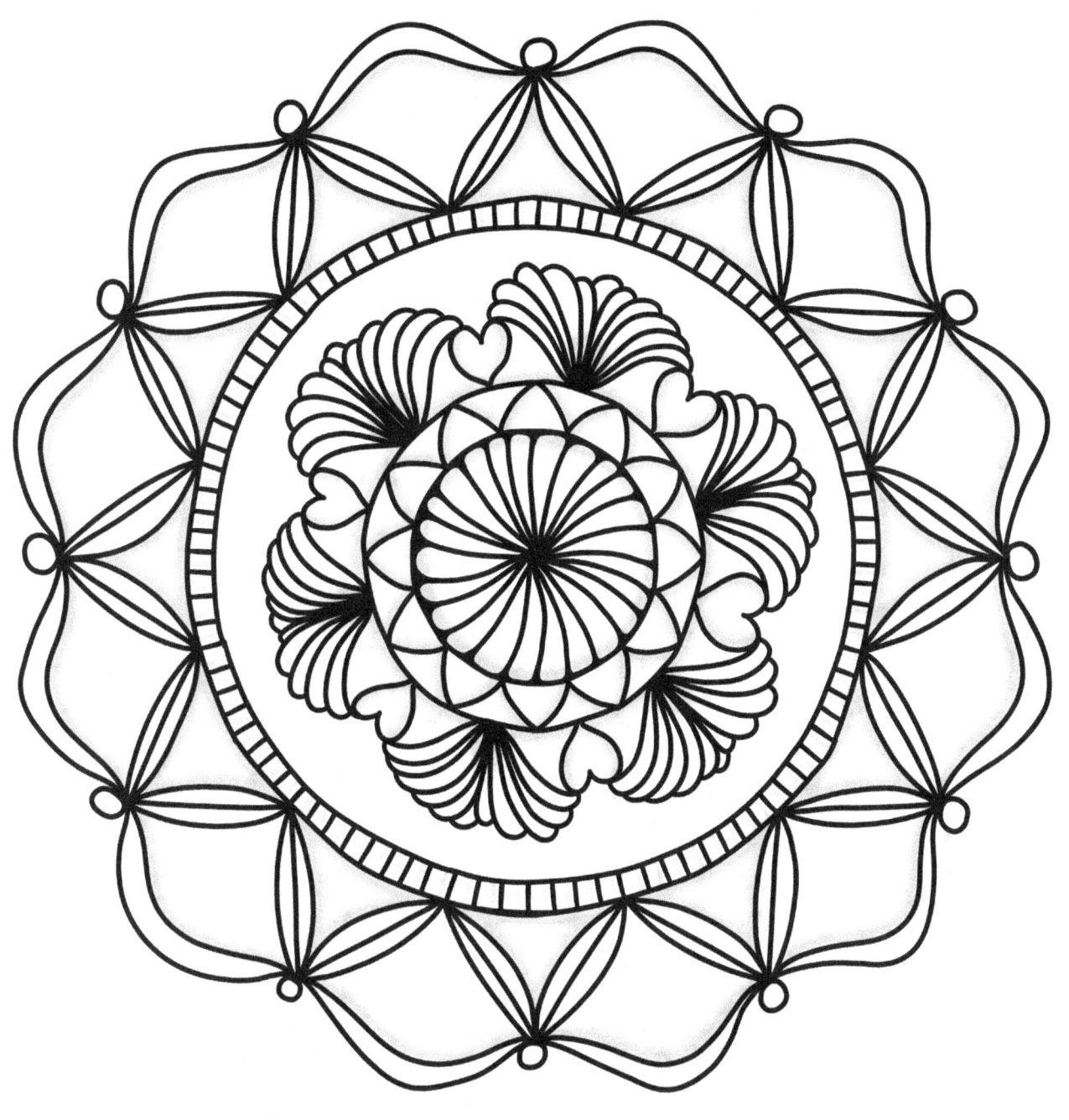

Date:_____   Colorist: _____
Media Type: _____
Media Test Area:

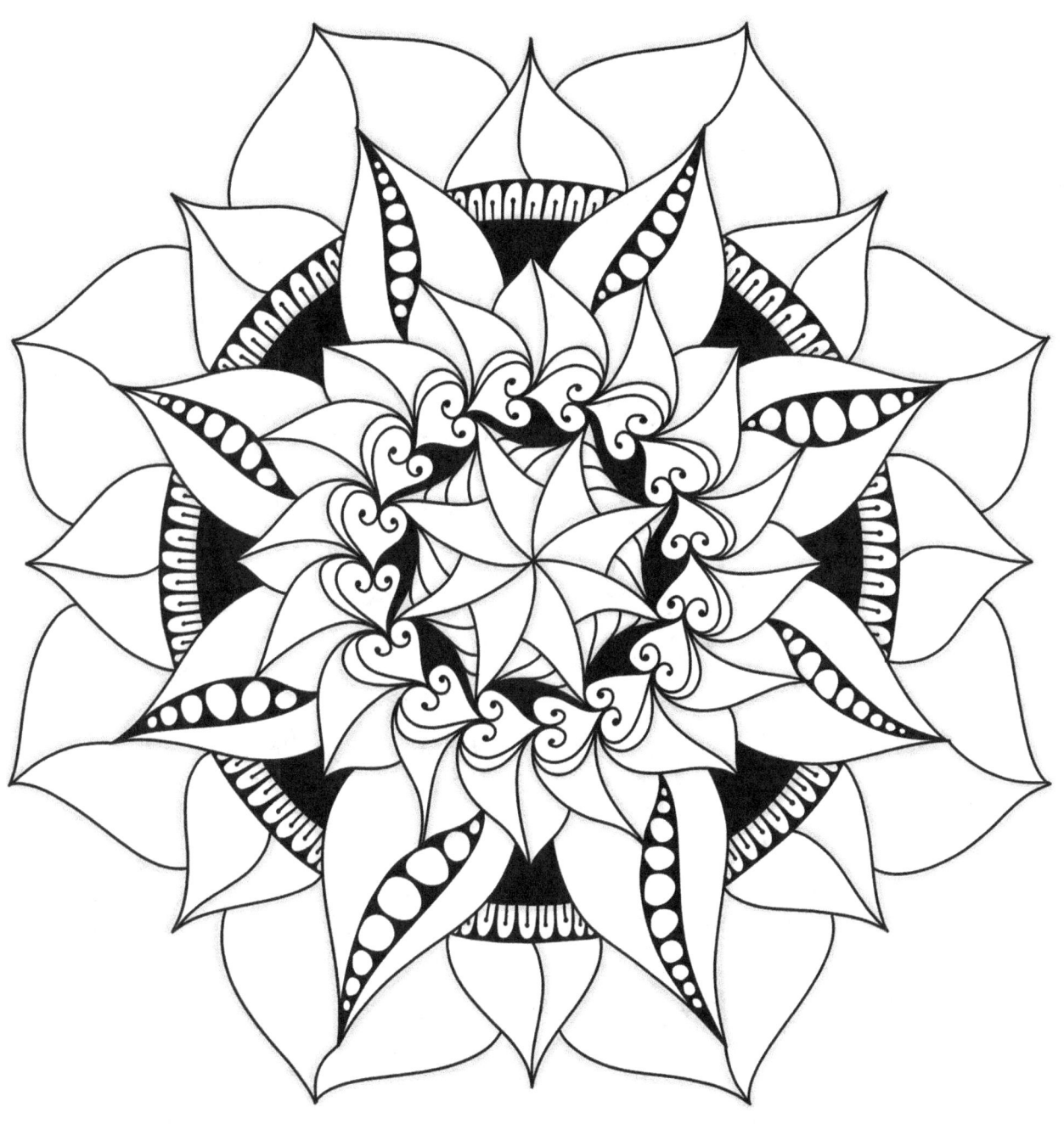

Date:_____ Colorist: _____
Media Type: _____
Media Test Area:

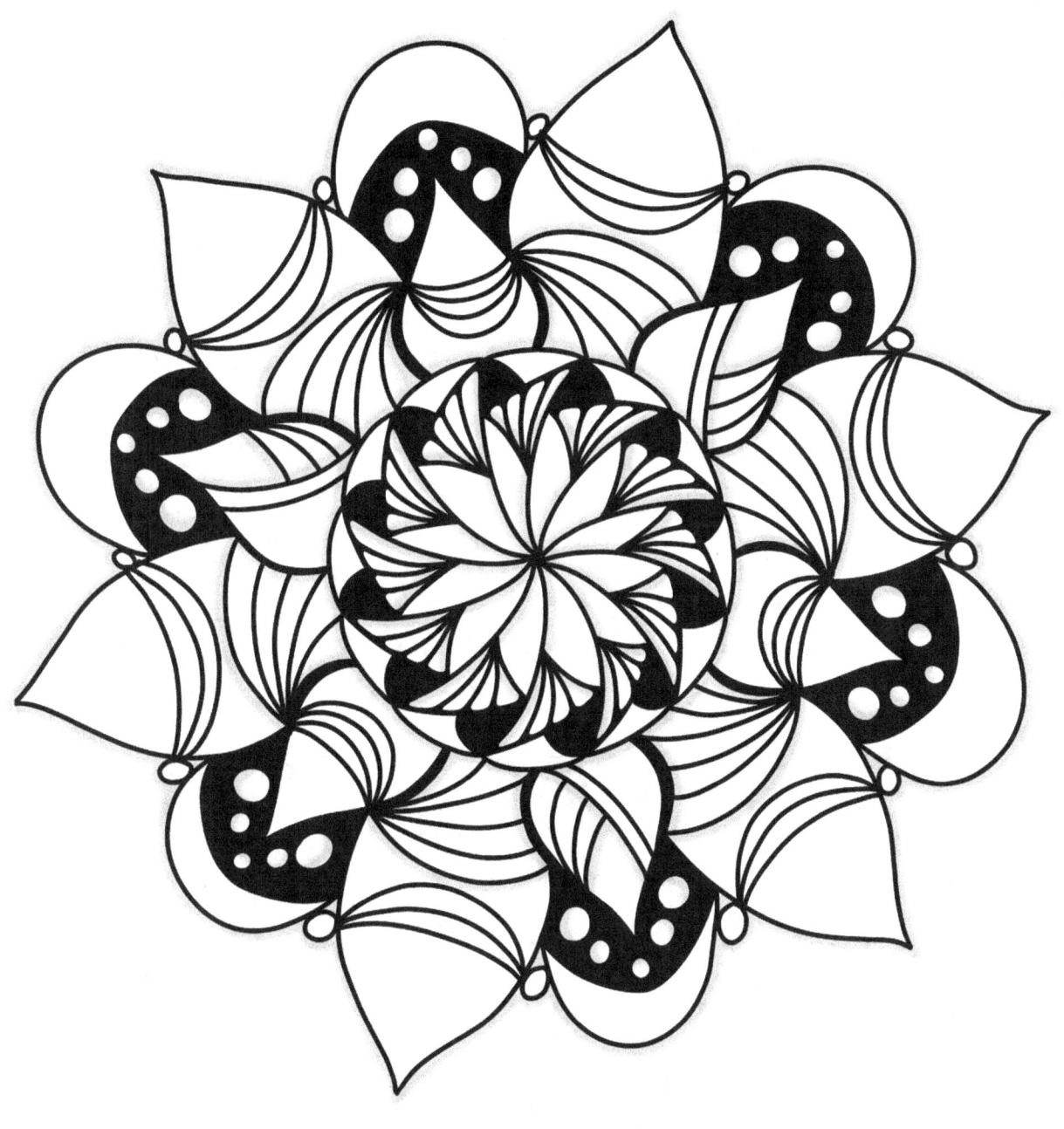

Date:_____ Colorist:_____
Media Type: _____
Media Test Area:

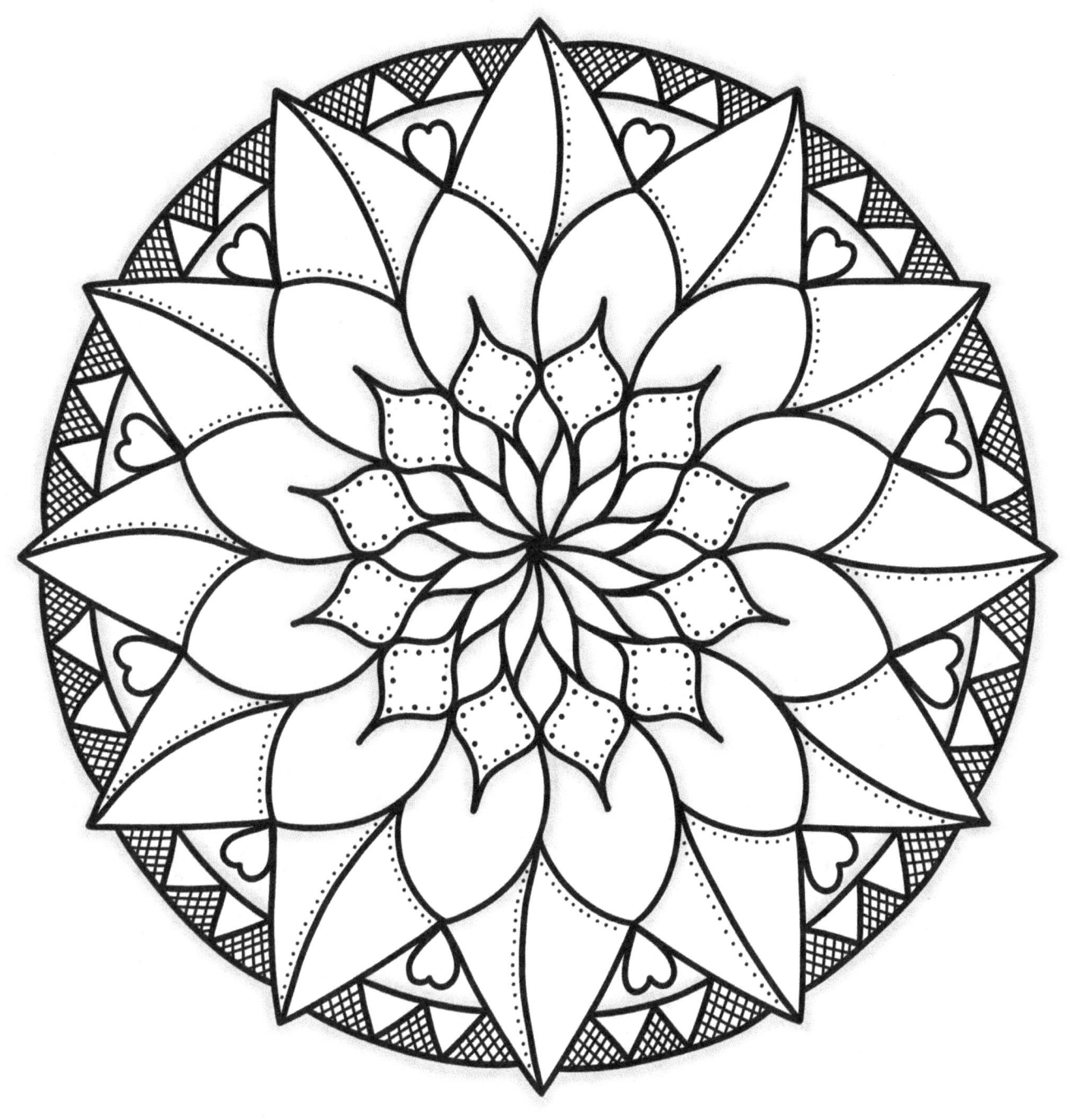

Date:_____ Colorist: _____
Media Type: _____
Media Test Area:

Date:_____   Colorist: _____
Media Type: _____
Media Test Area:

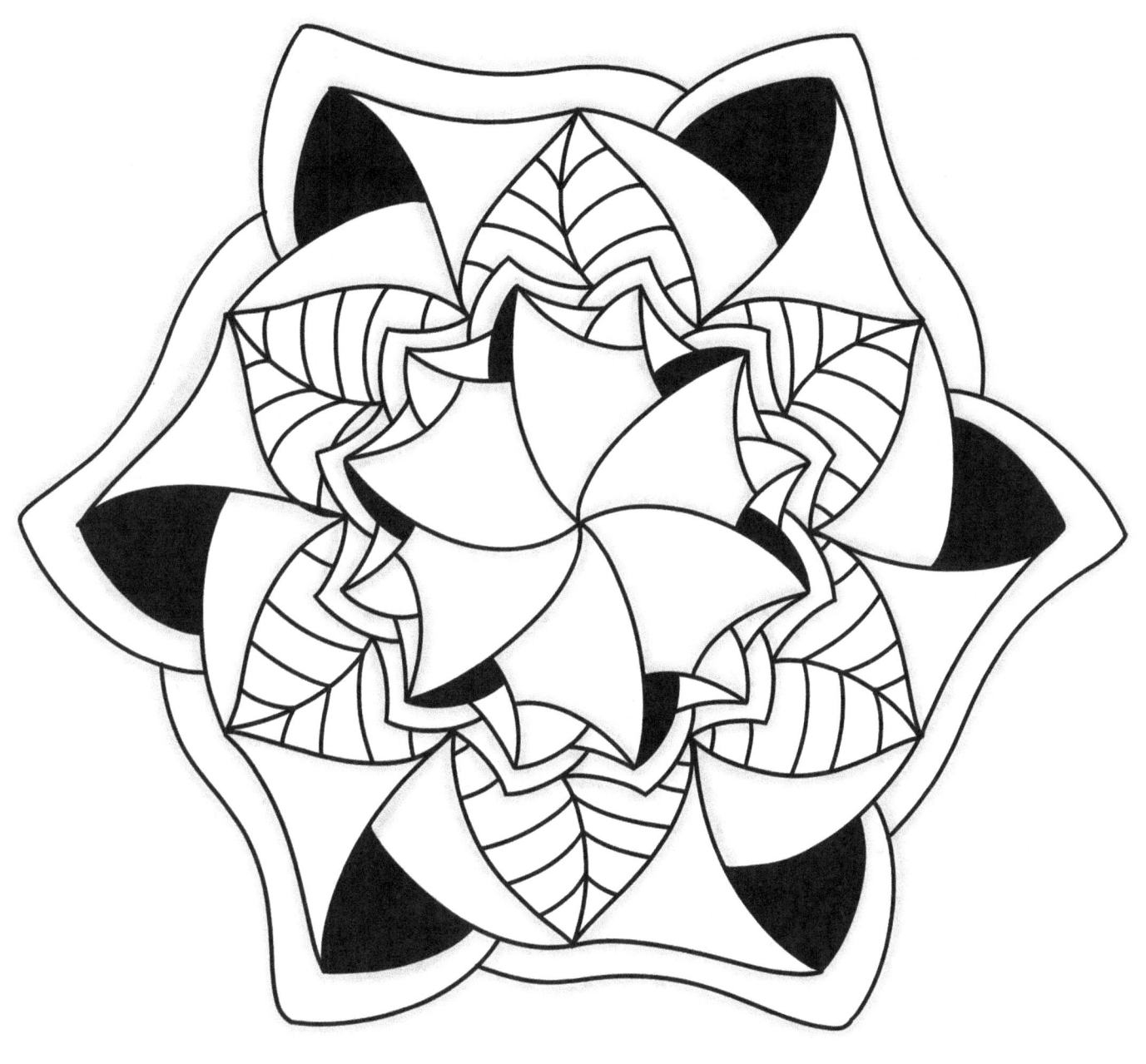

Date:_____   Colorist: _____
Media Type: _____
Media Test Area:

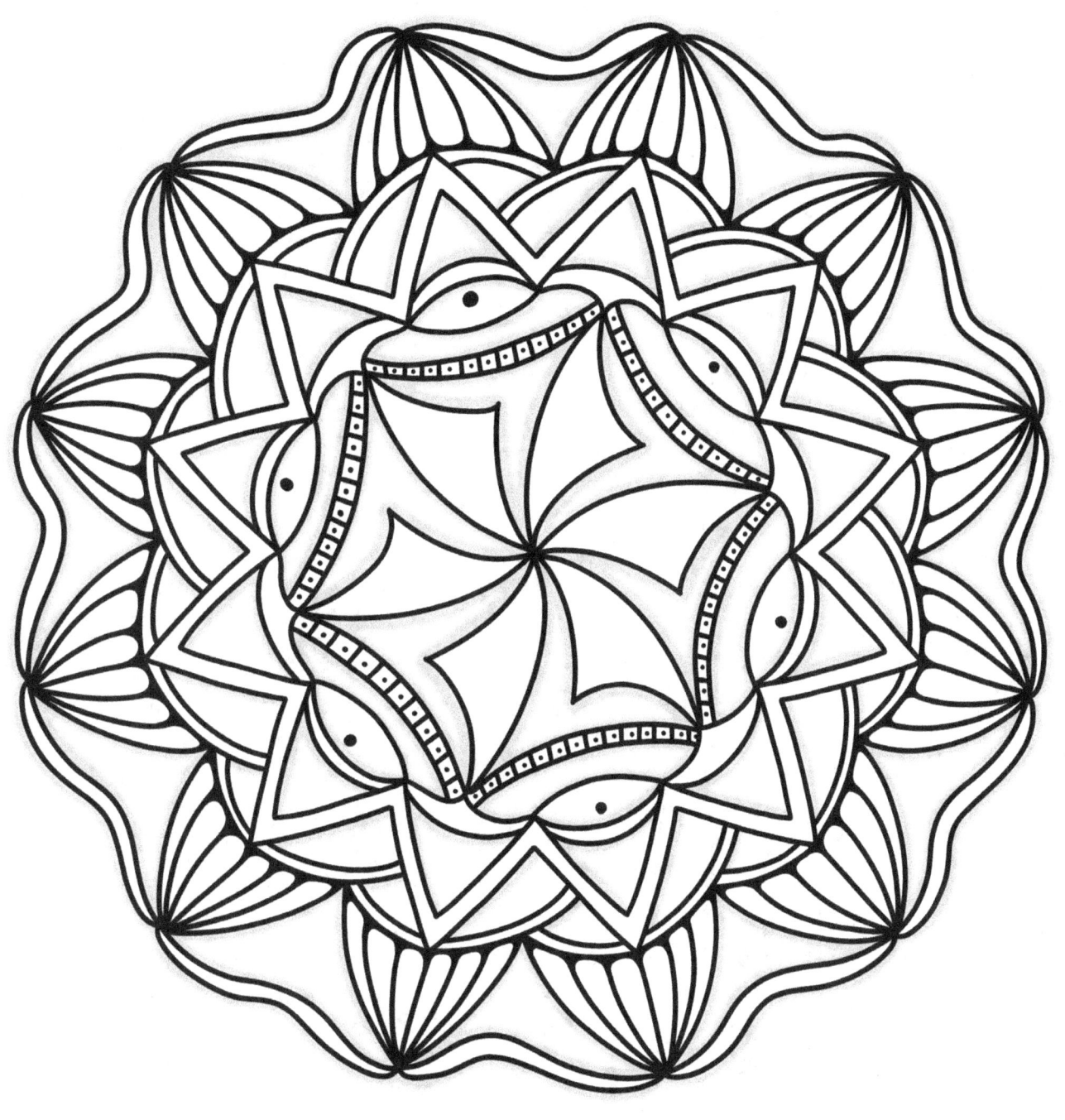

Date:_____ Colorist:_____
Media Type: _____
Media Test Area:

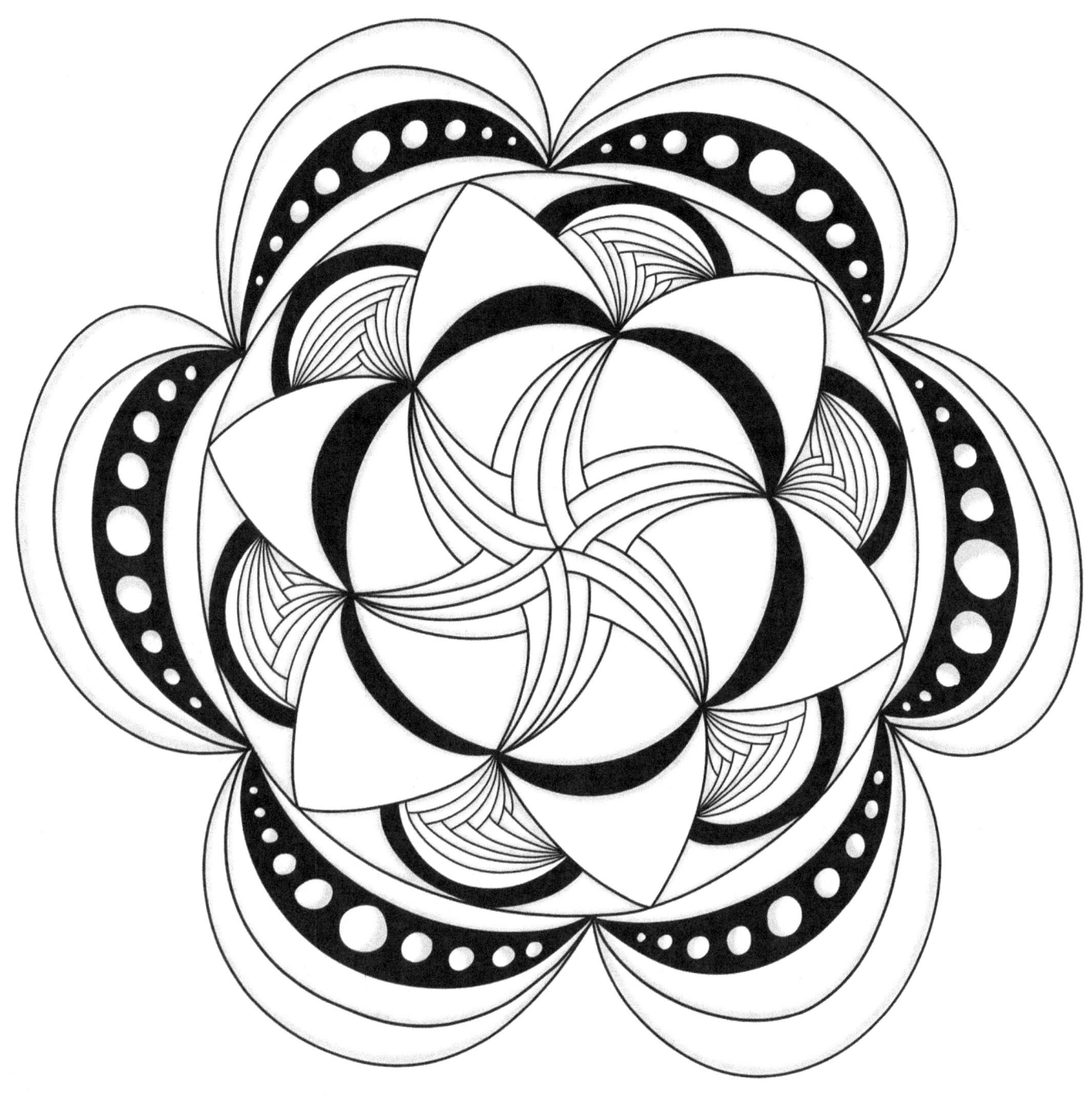

Date:_____   Colorist: _____
Media Type: _____
Media Test Area:

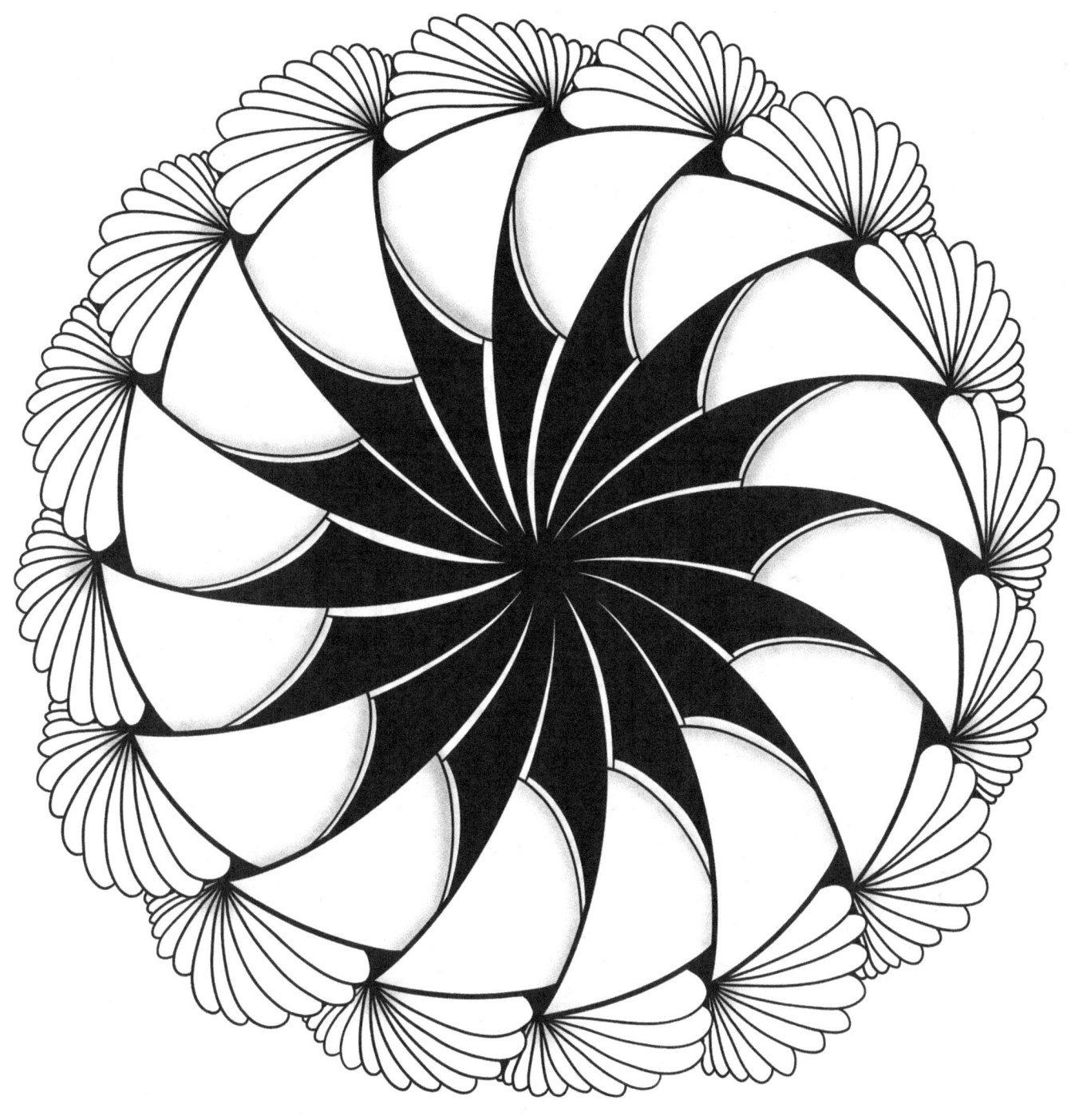

Date:_____ Colorist: _____
Media Type: _____
Media Test Area:

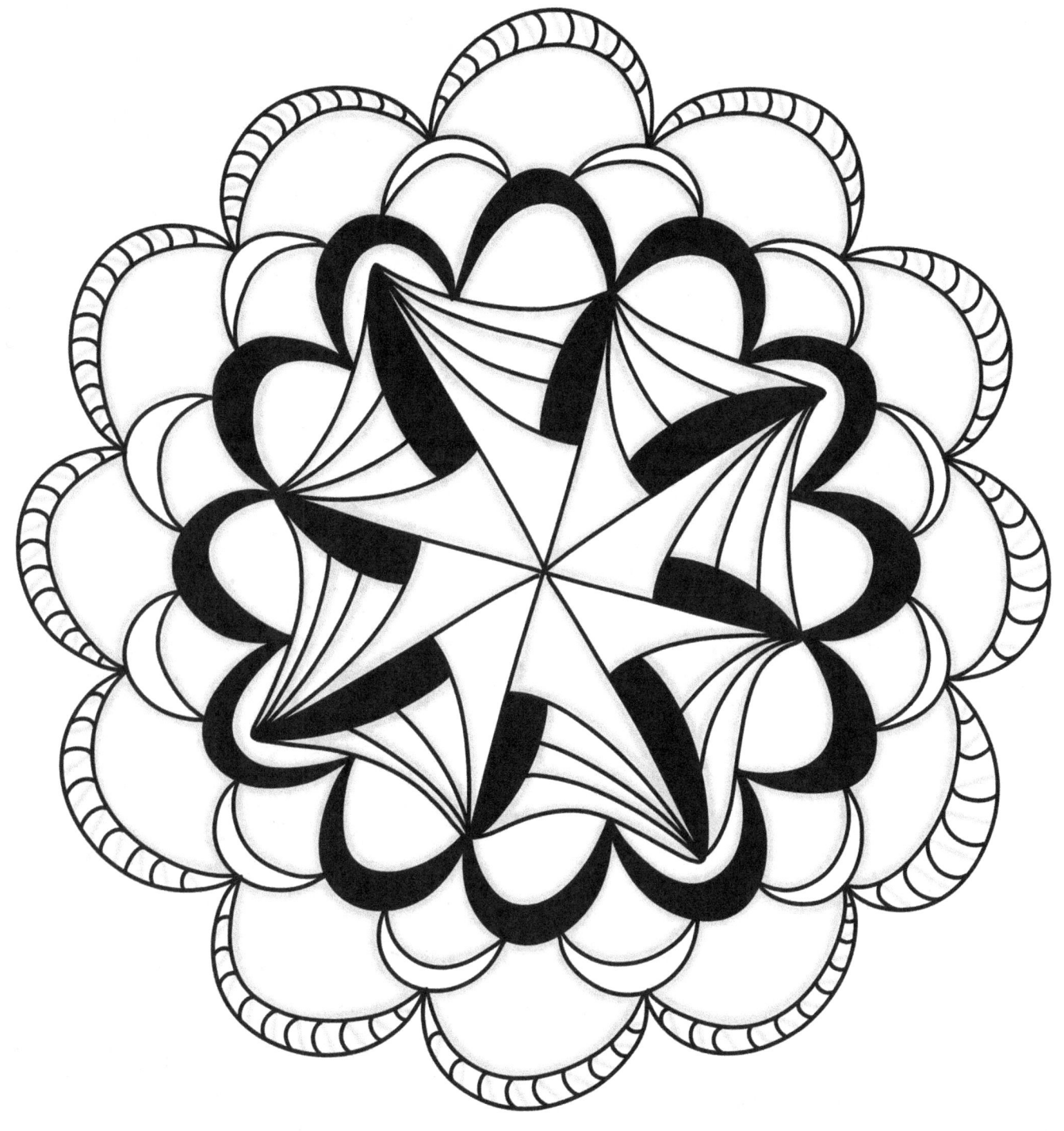

Date:_____   Colorist: _____
Media Type: _____
Media Test Area:

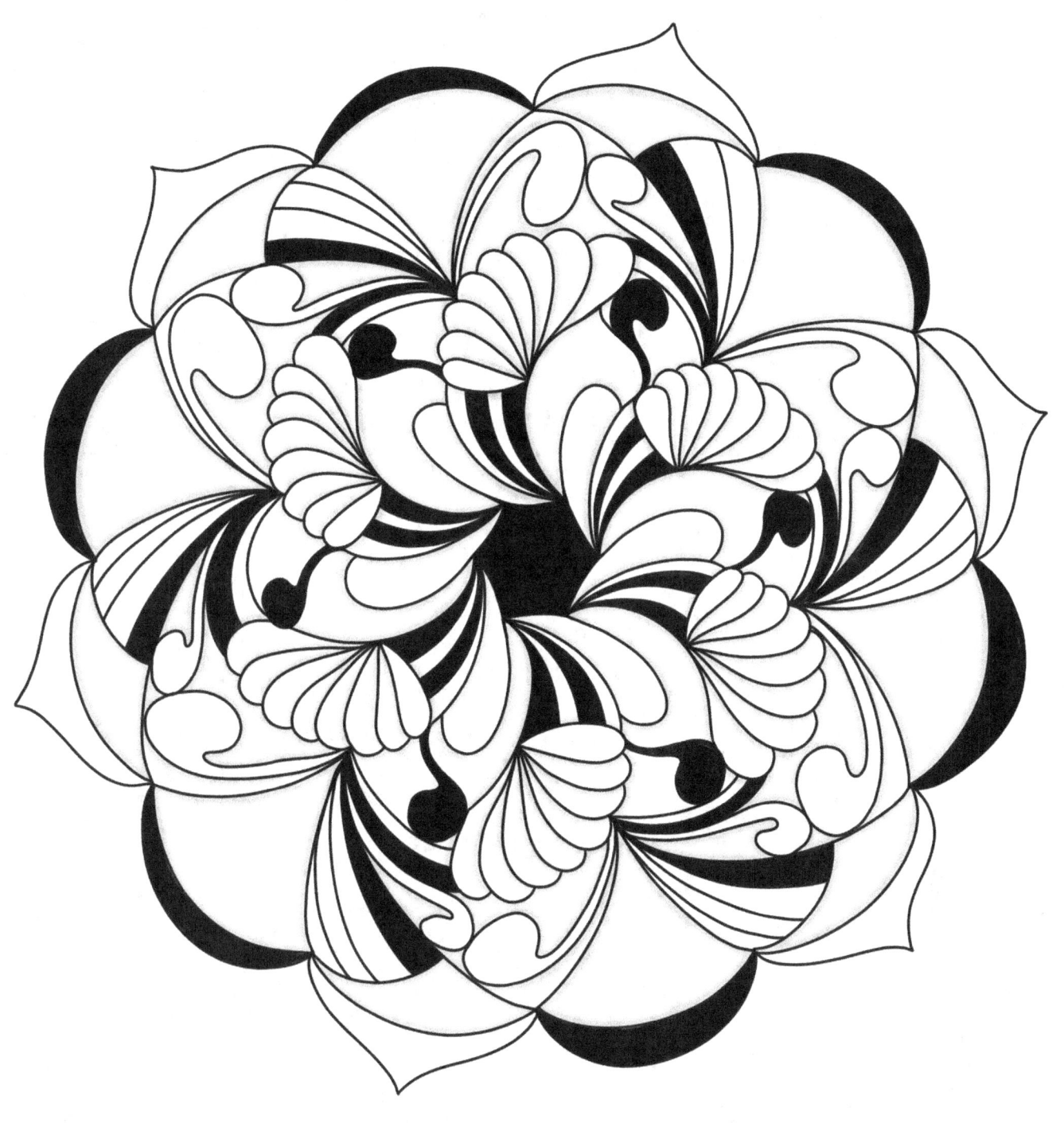

Date:_____   Colorist: _____
Media Type: _____
Media Test Area:

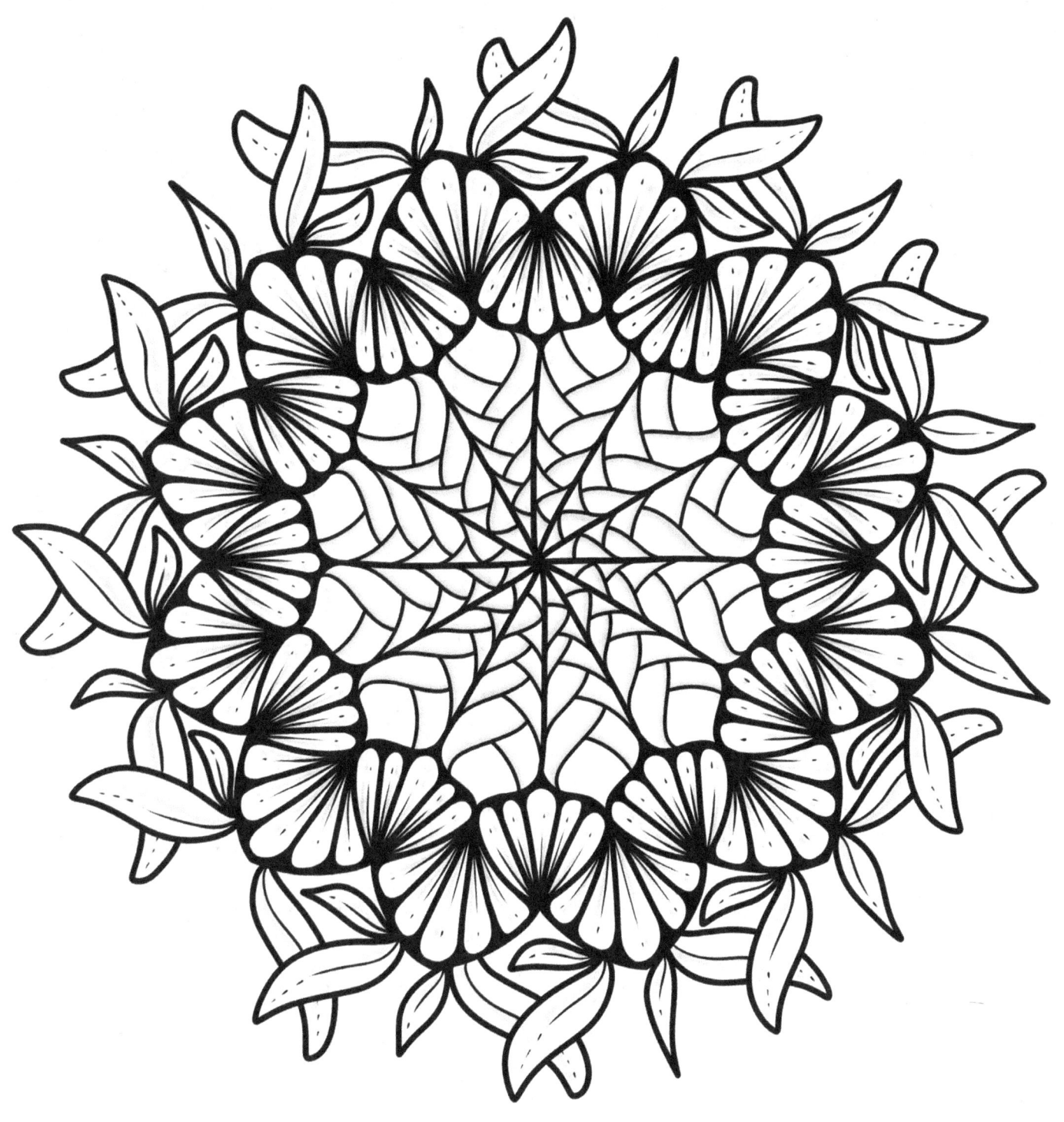

Date:_____ Colorist: _____
Media Type: _____
Media Test Area:

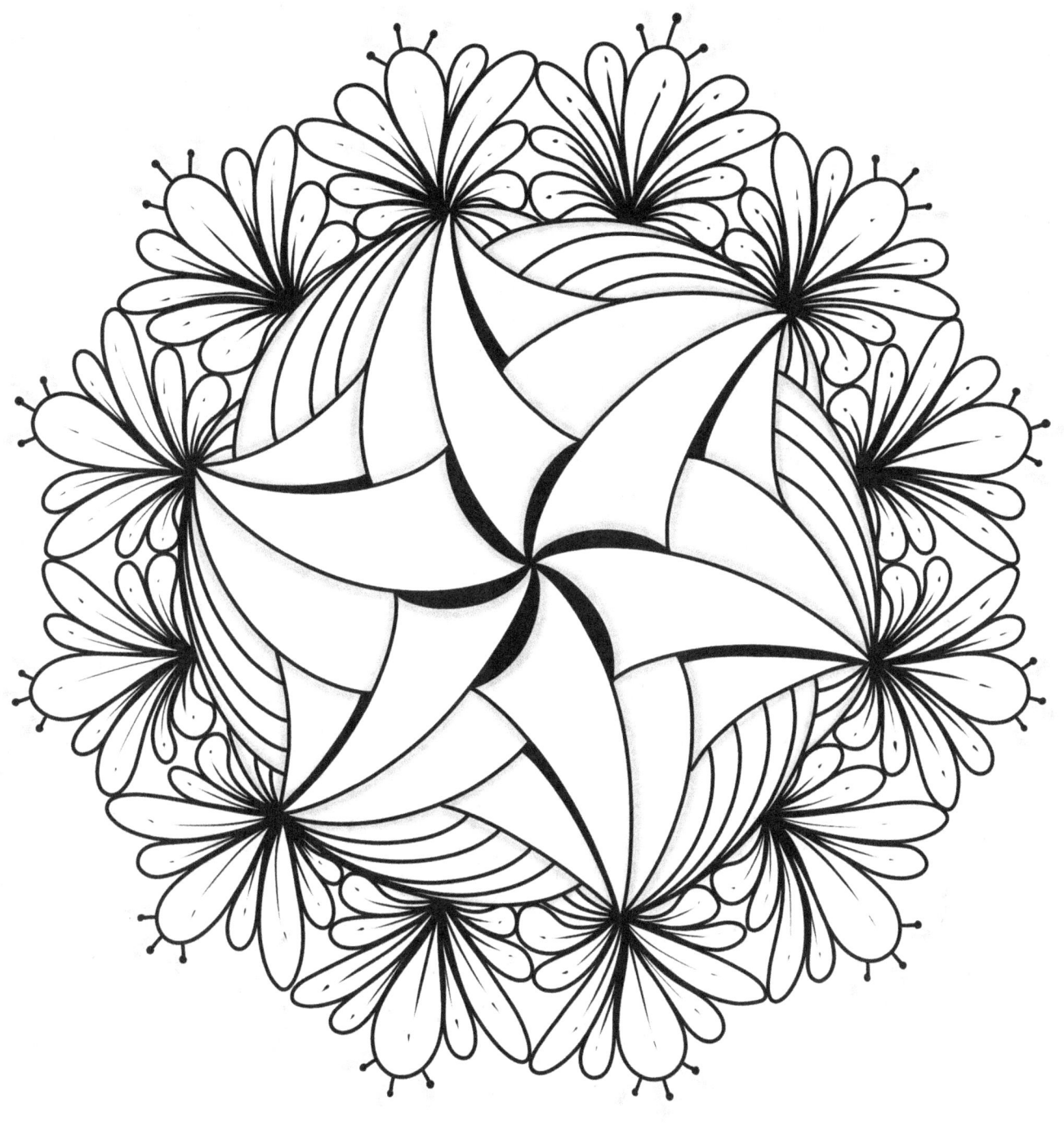

Date:_____ Colorist: _____
Media Type: _____
Media Test Area:

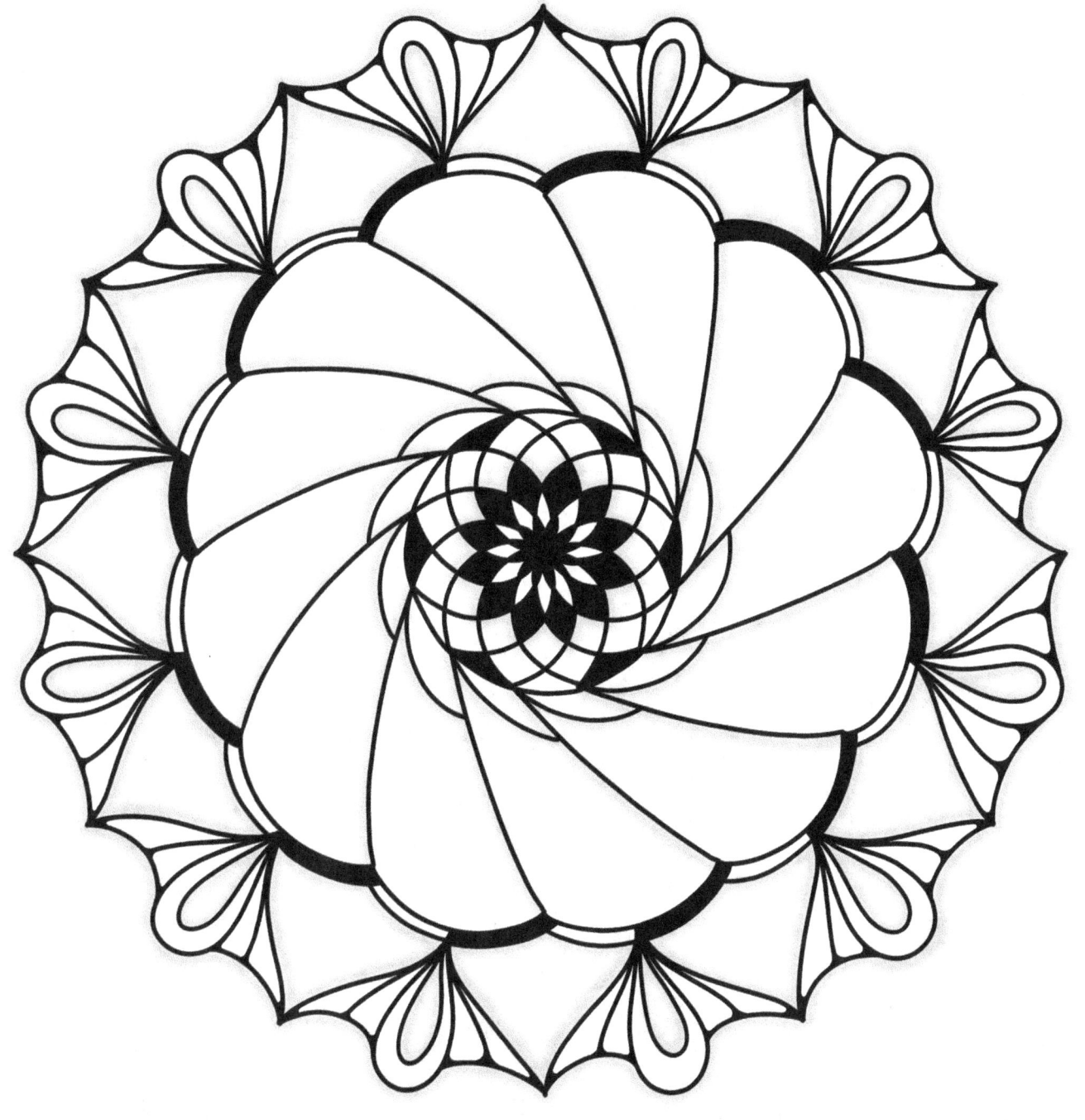

Date:_____   Colorist:_____
Media Type: _____
Media Test Area:

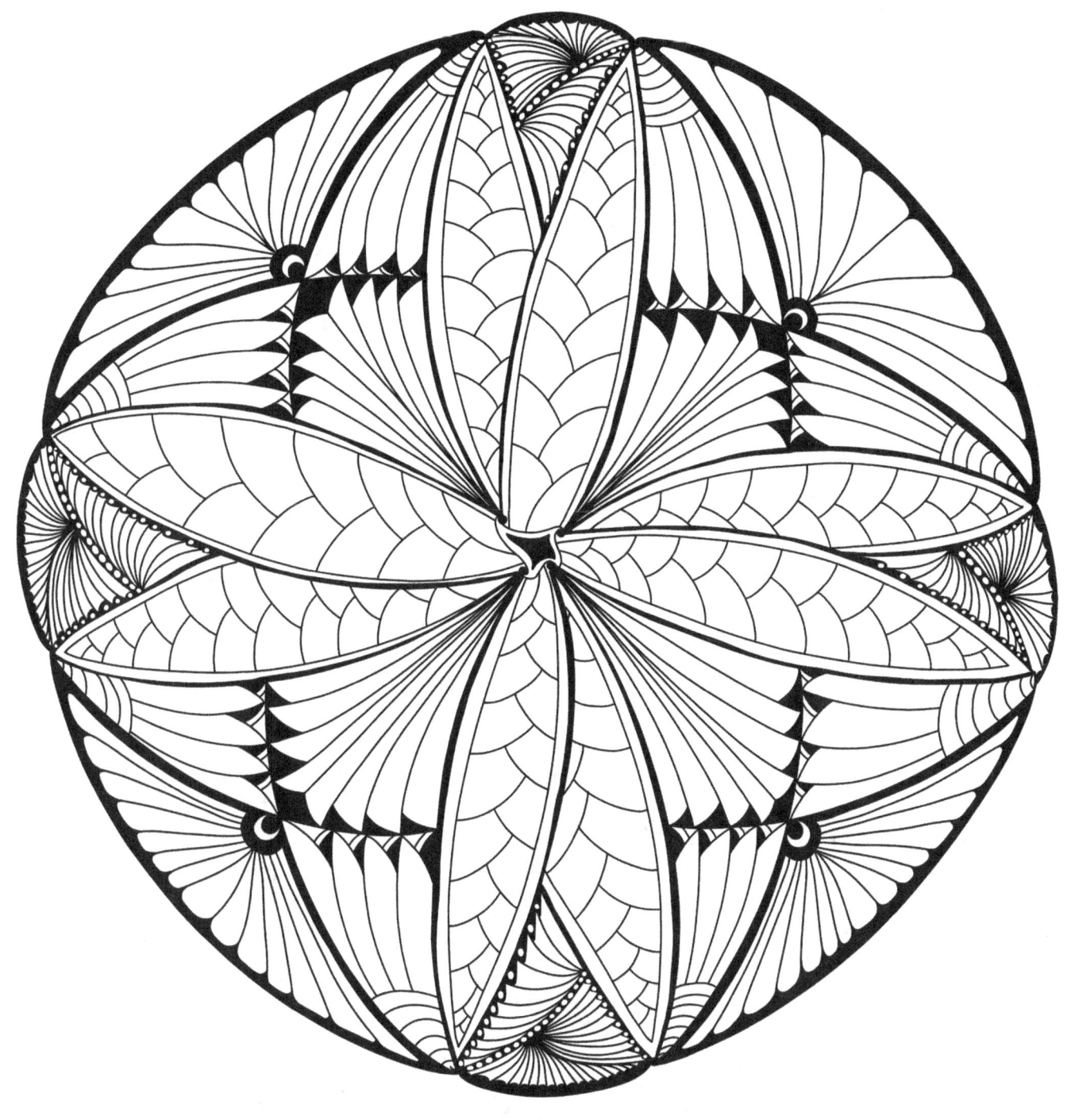

Date:_____   Colorist: _____
Media Type: _____
Media Test Area:

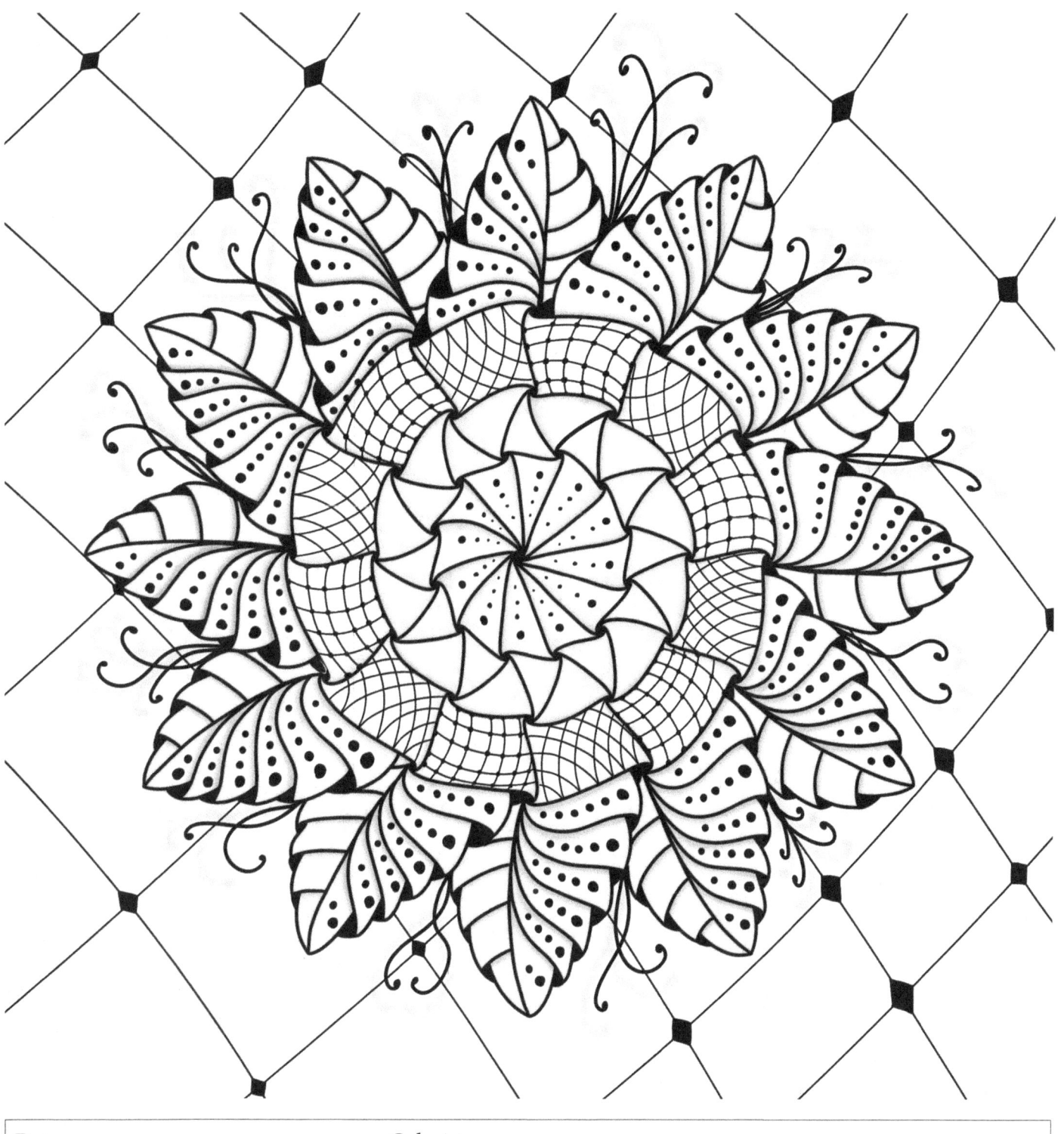

Date:_____ Colorist: _____
Media Type: _____
Media Test Area:

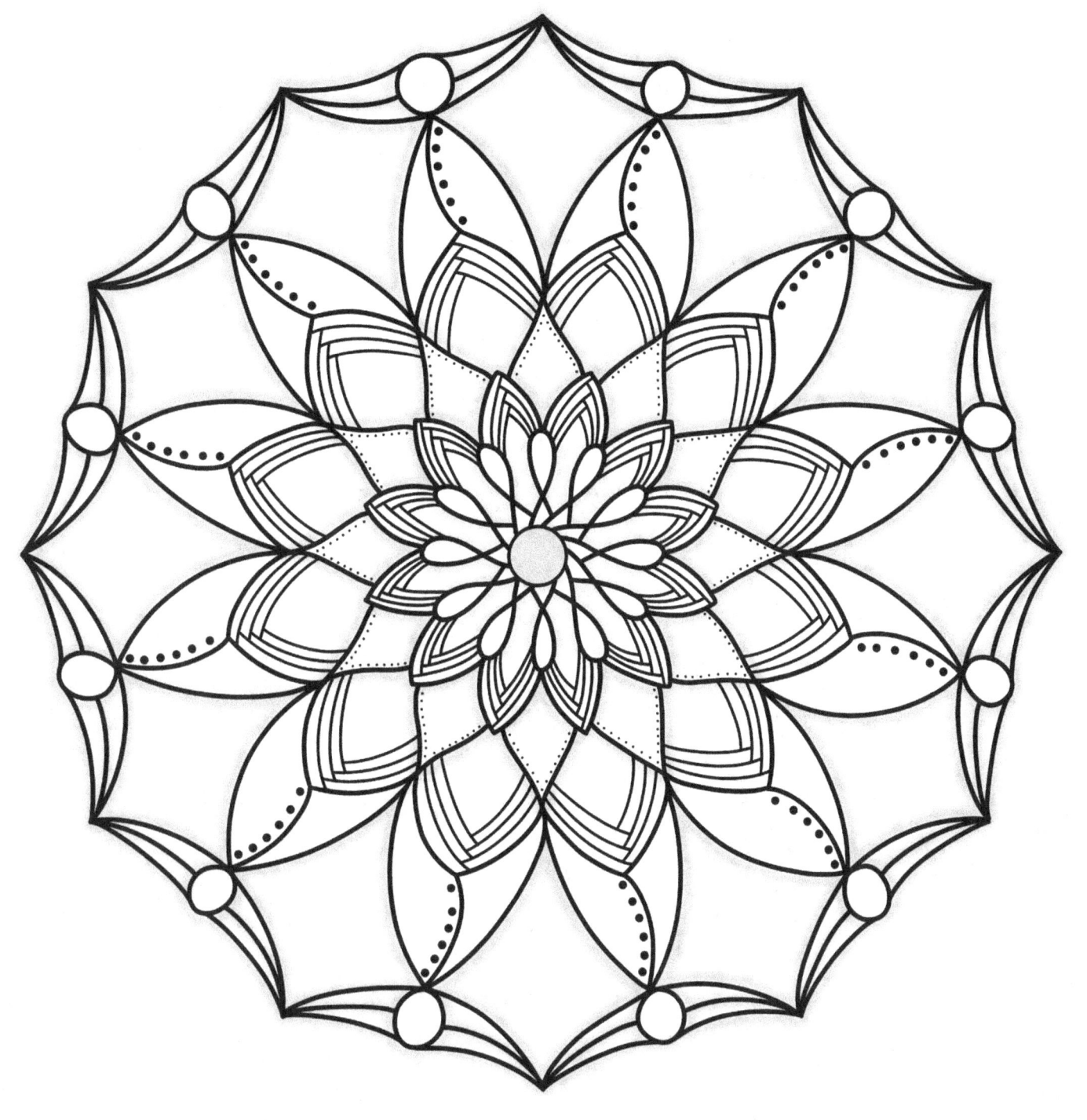

Date:_____ Colorist: _____
Media Type: _____
Media Test Area:

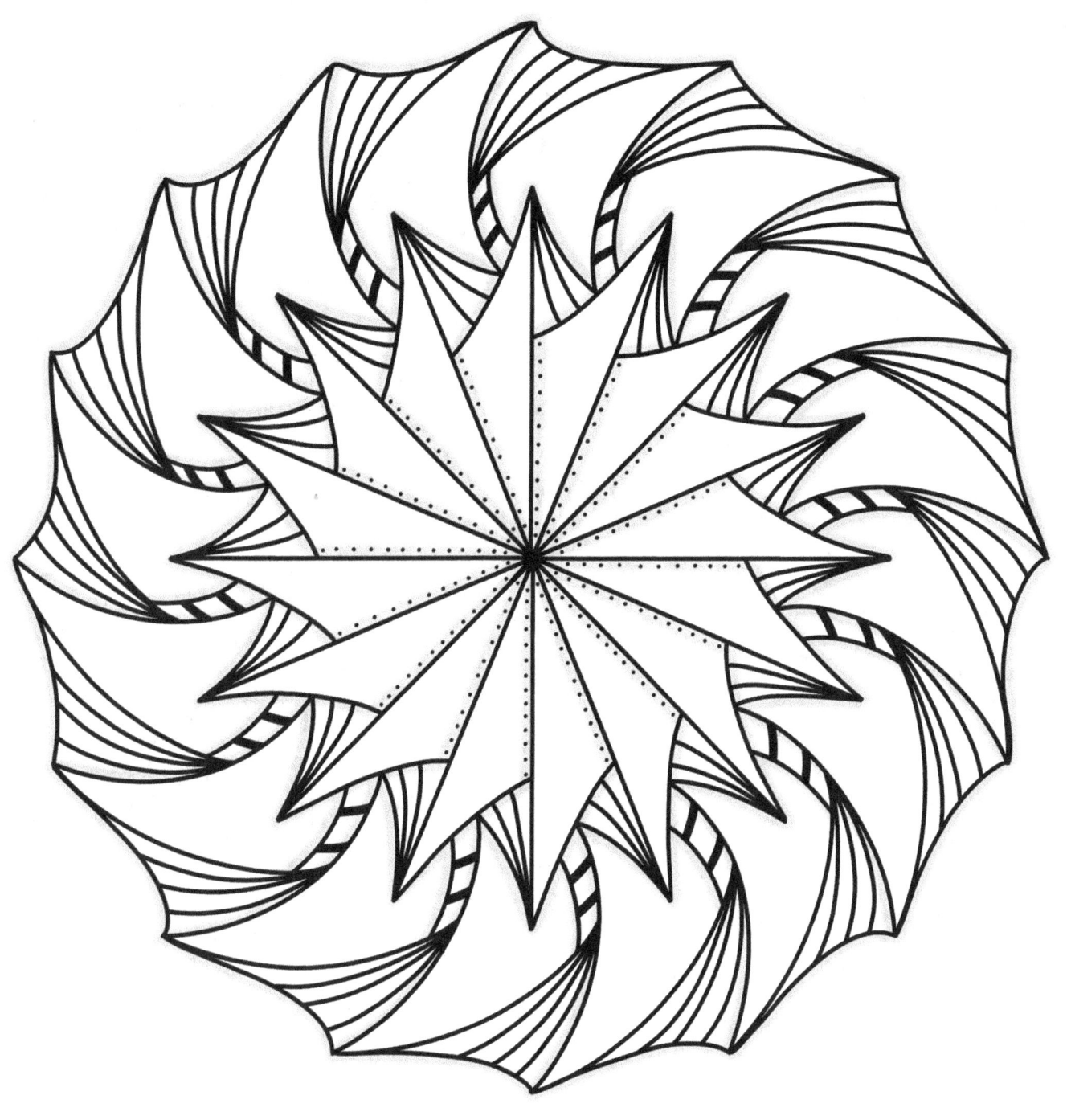

Date:_____   Colorist: _____
Media Type: _____
Media Test Area:

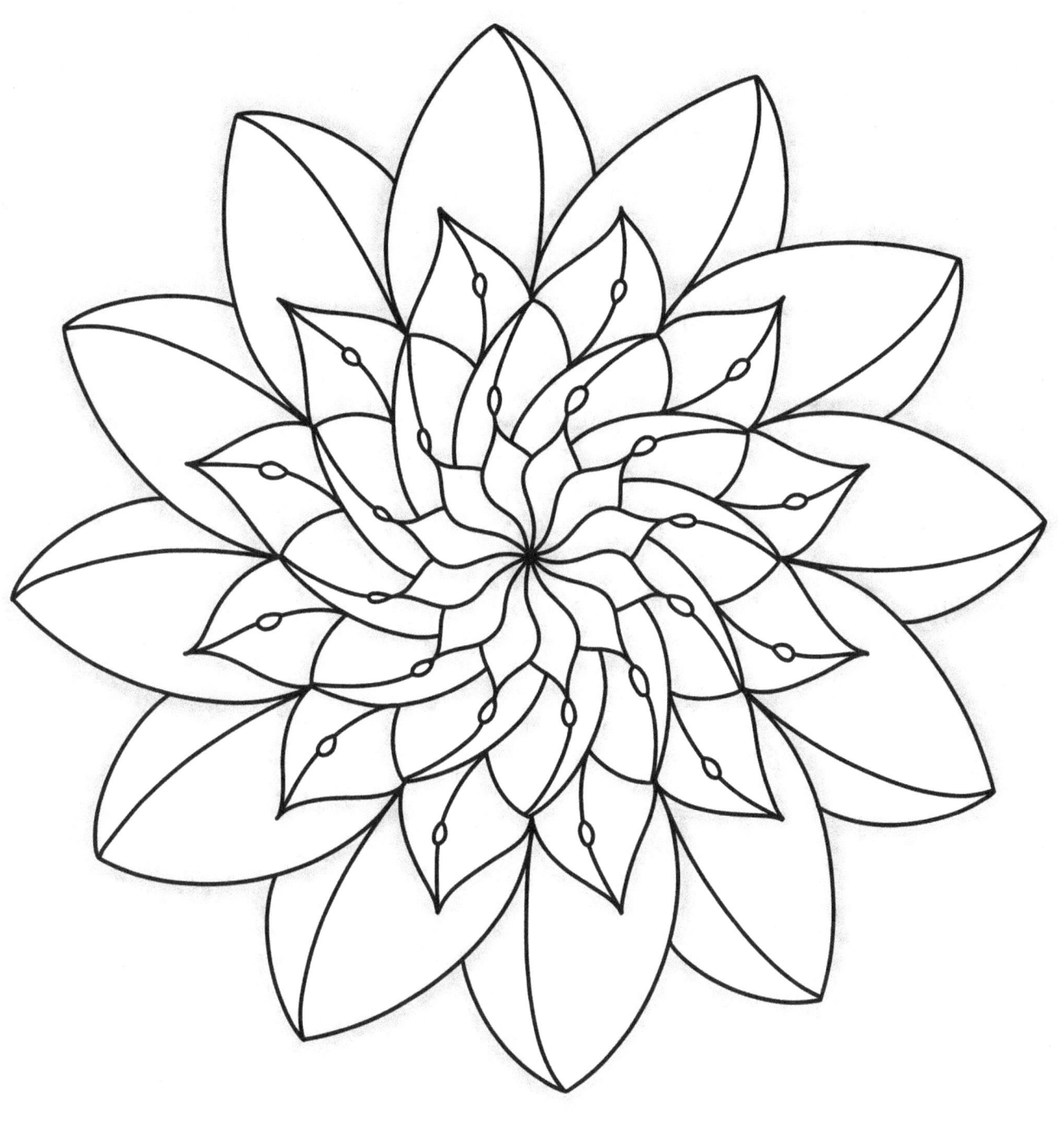

Date:_____   Colorist:_____
Media Type: _____
Media Test Area:

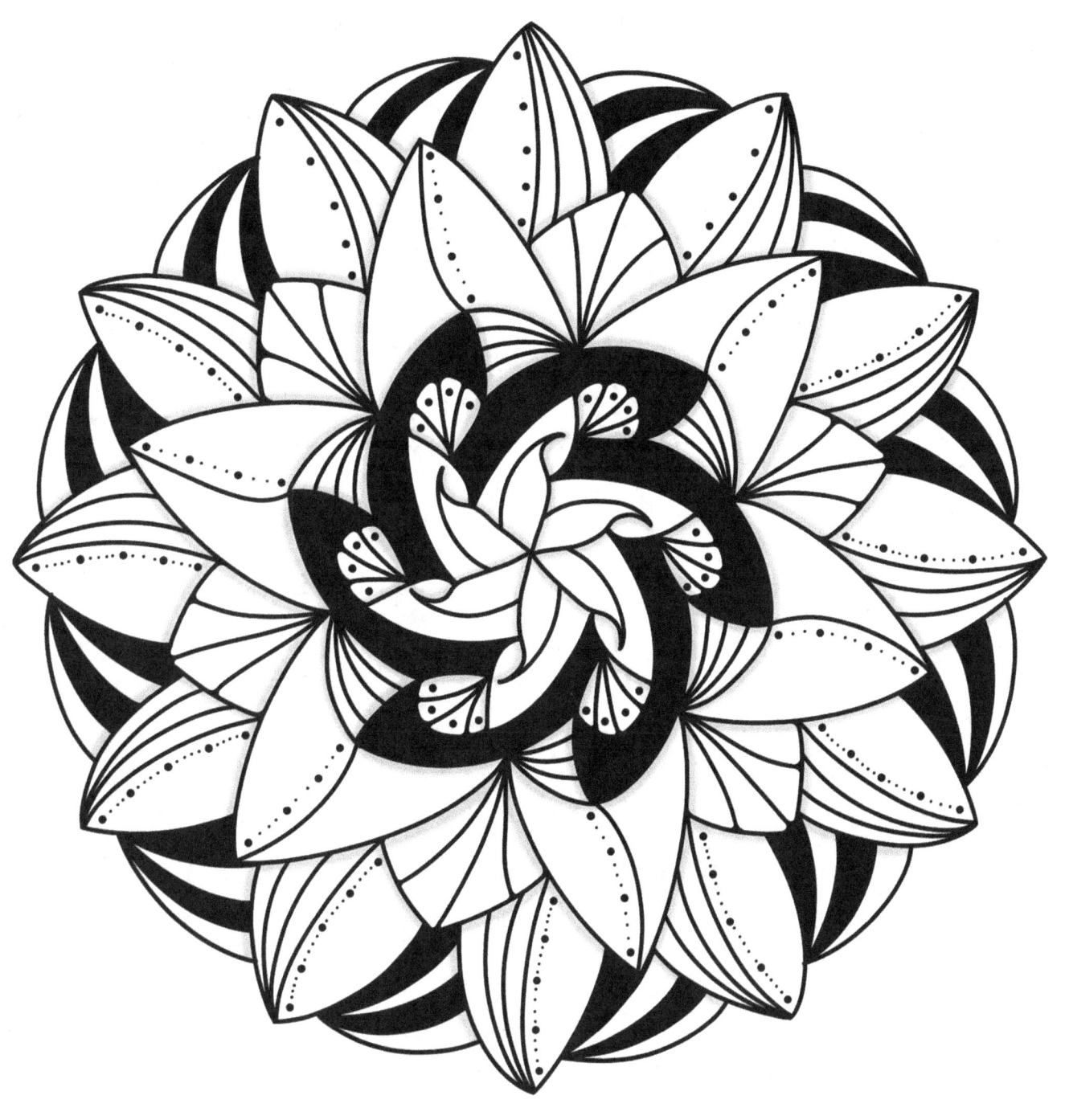

Date:_____   Colorist:_____
Media Type: _____
Media Test Area:

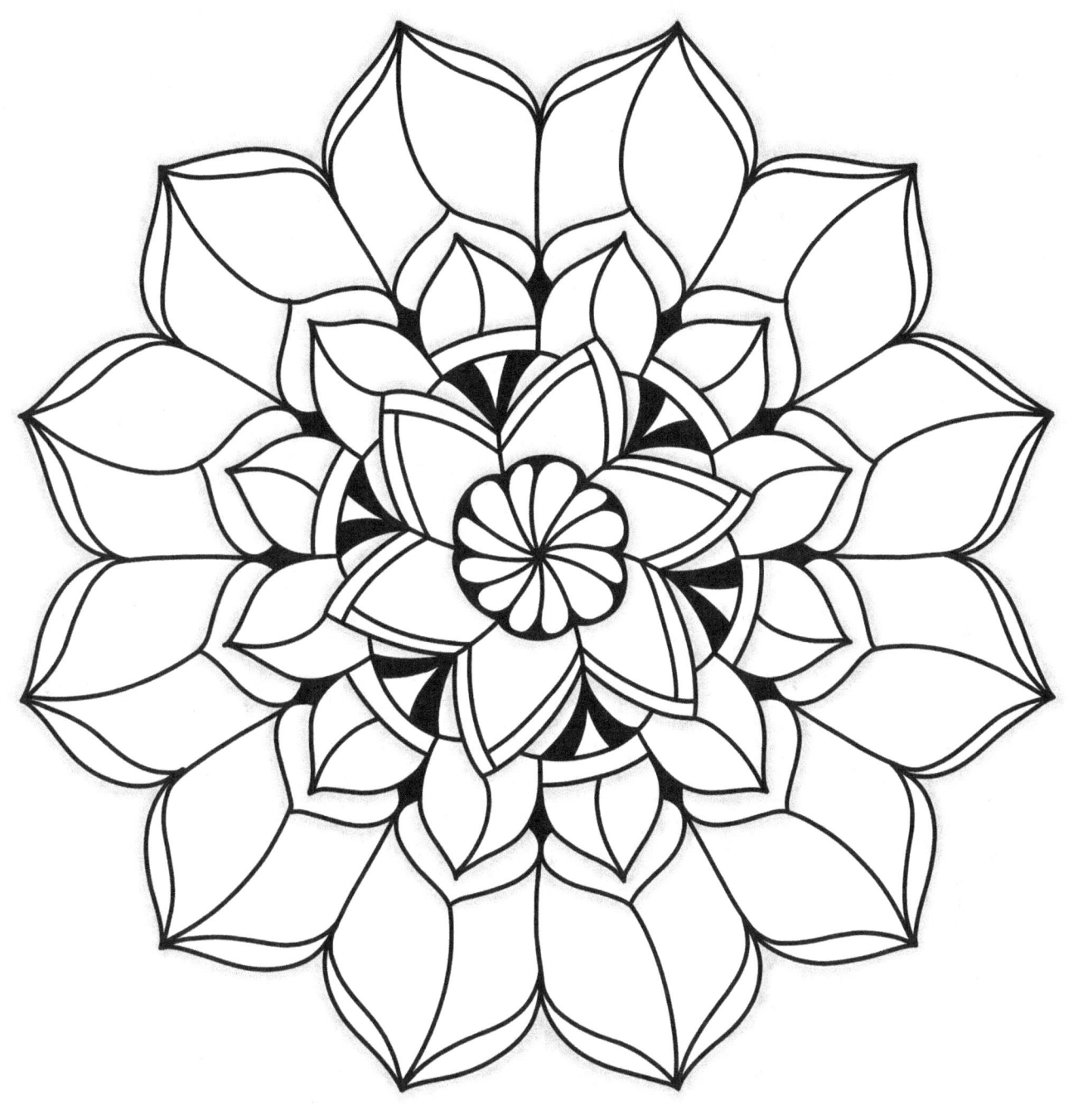

Date:_____ Colorist:_____
Media Type: _____
Media Test Area:

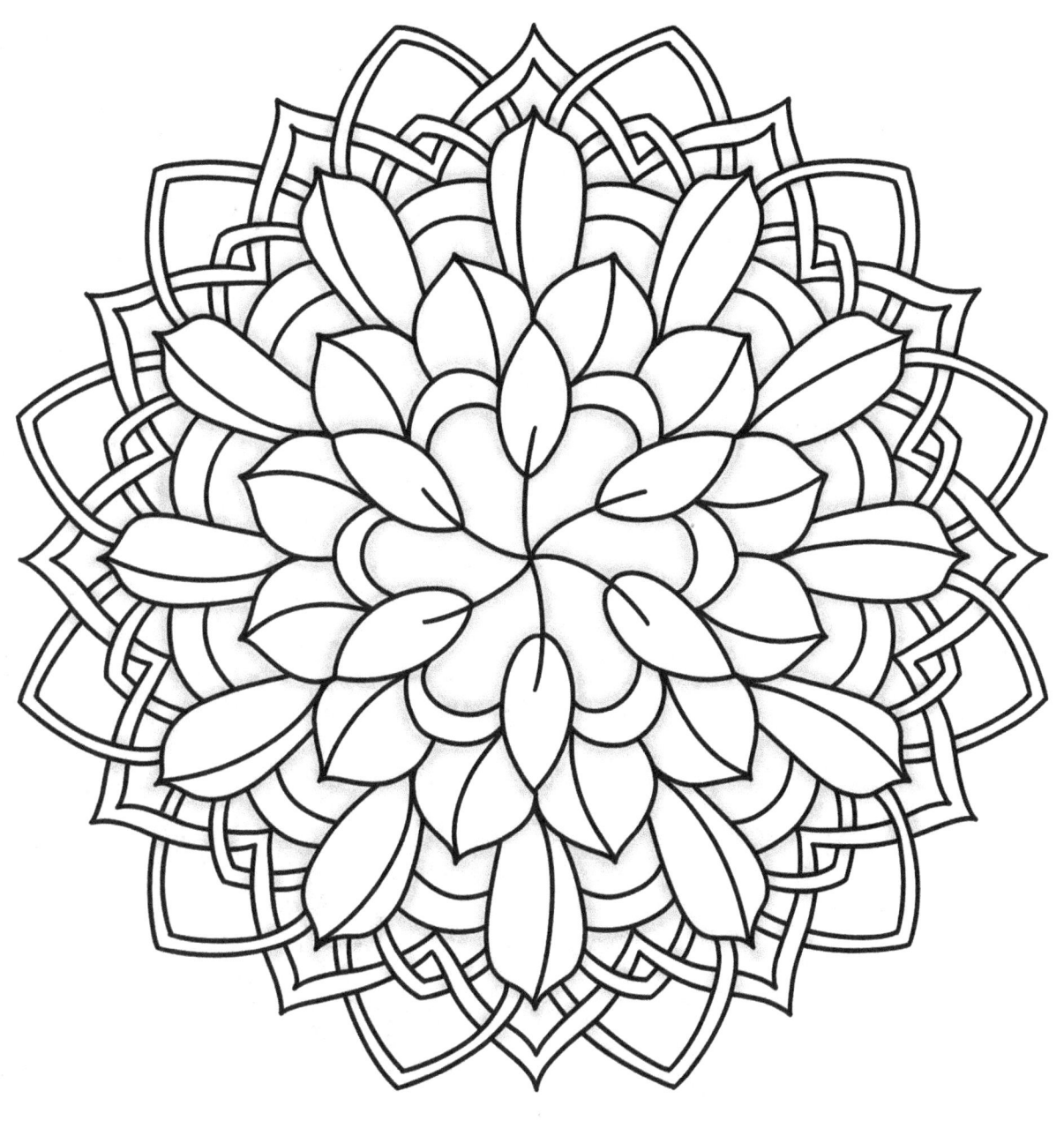

Date:_____   Colorist: _____
Media Type: _____
Media Test Area:

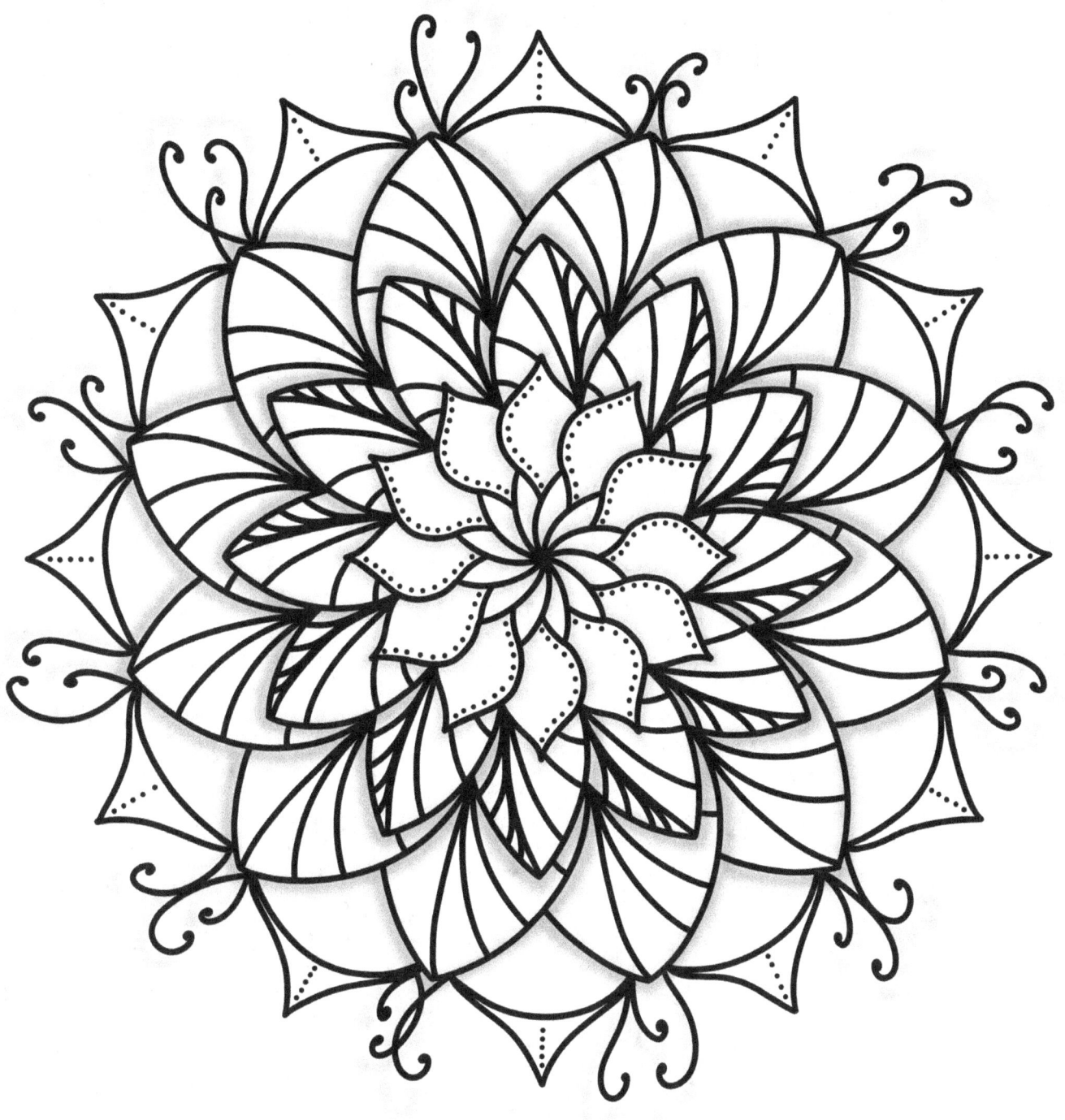

Date:_____   Colorist: _____
Media Type: _____
Media Test Area:

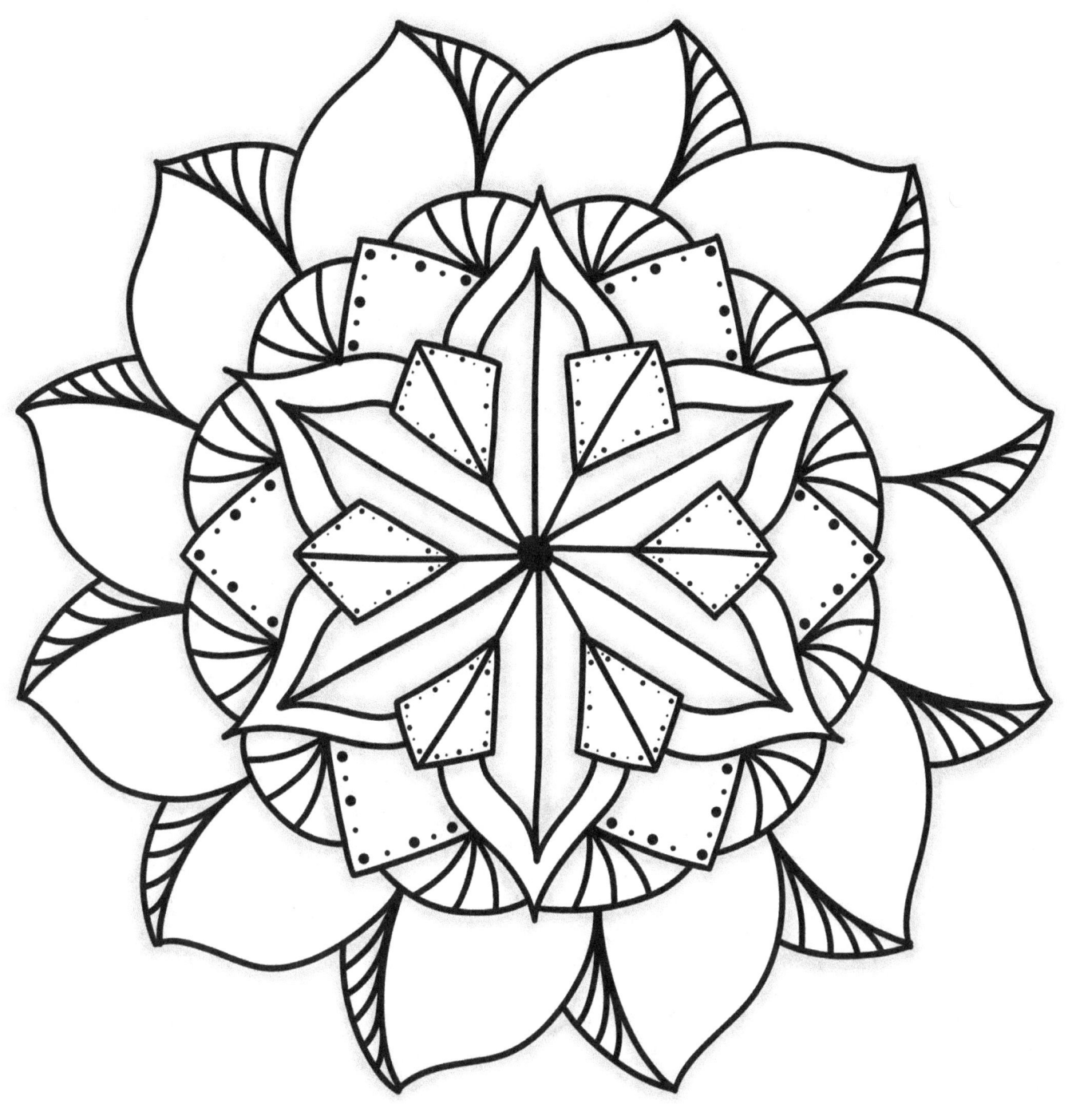

Date:_____   Colorist: _____
Media Type: _____
Media Test Area:

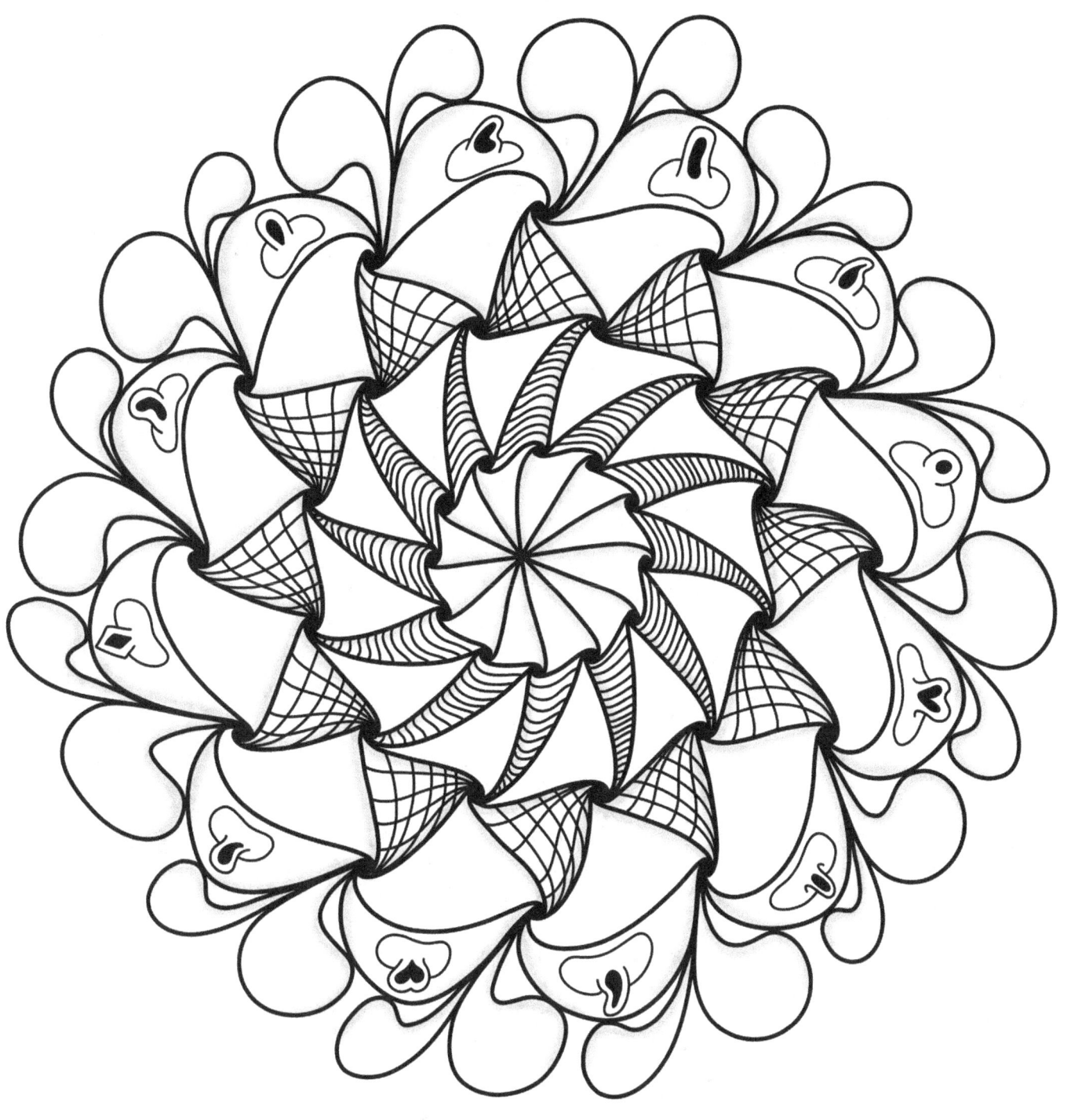

Date:_____ Colorist: _____
Media Type: _____
Media Test Area:

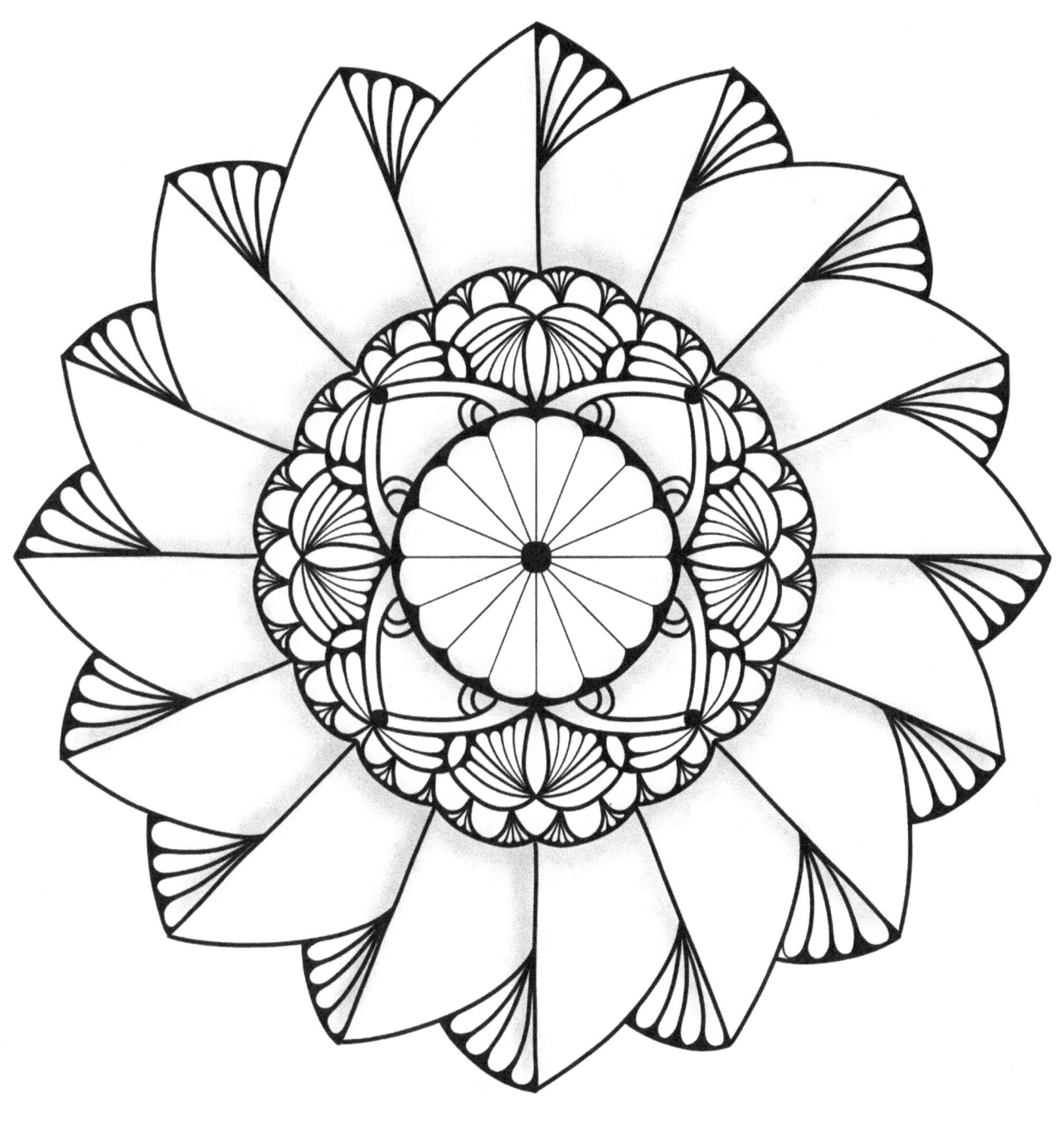

Date:_____ Colorist: _____
Media Type: _____
Media Test Area:

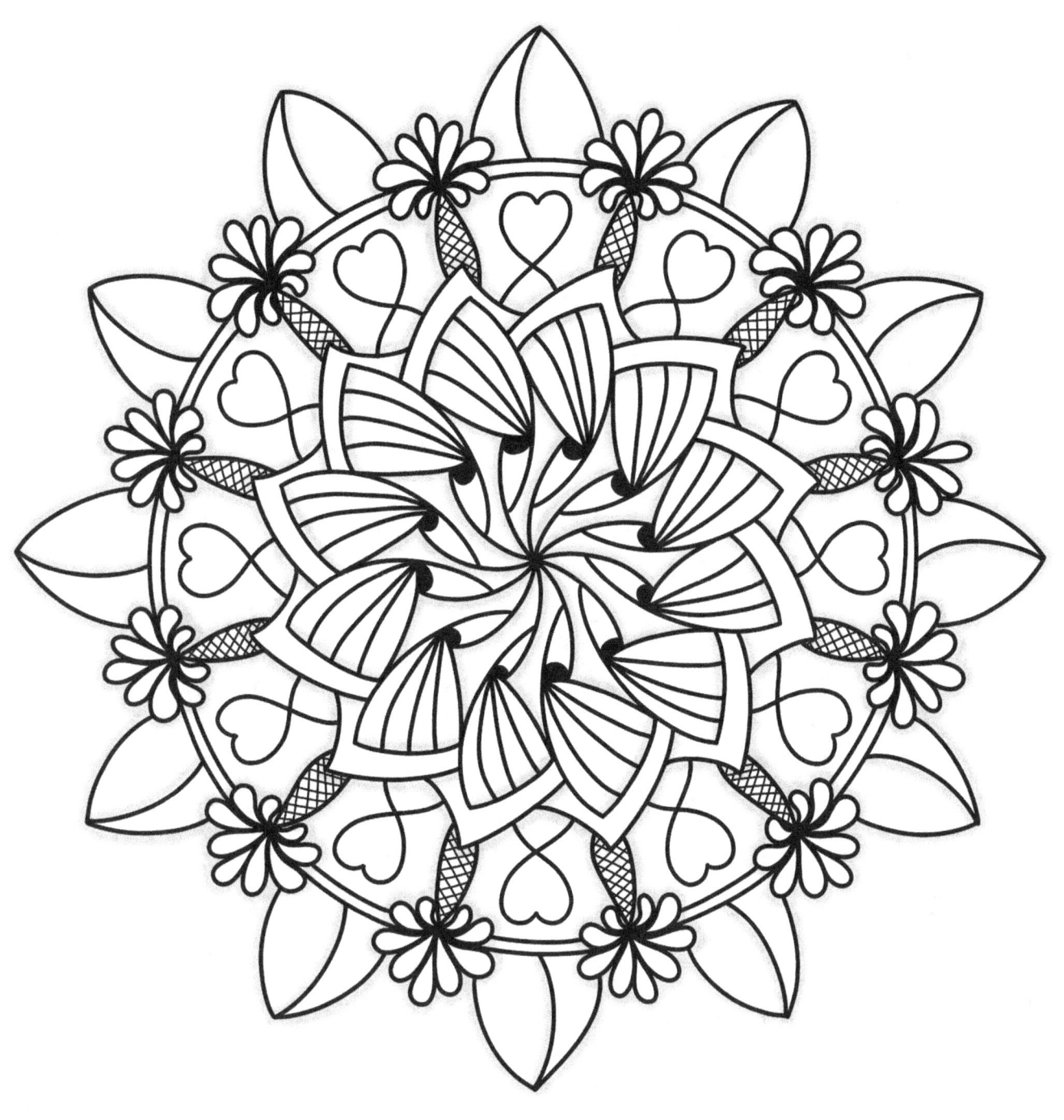

Date:_____ Colorist: _____
Media Type: _____
Media Test Area:

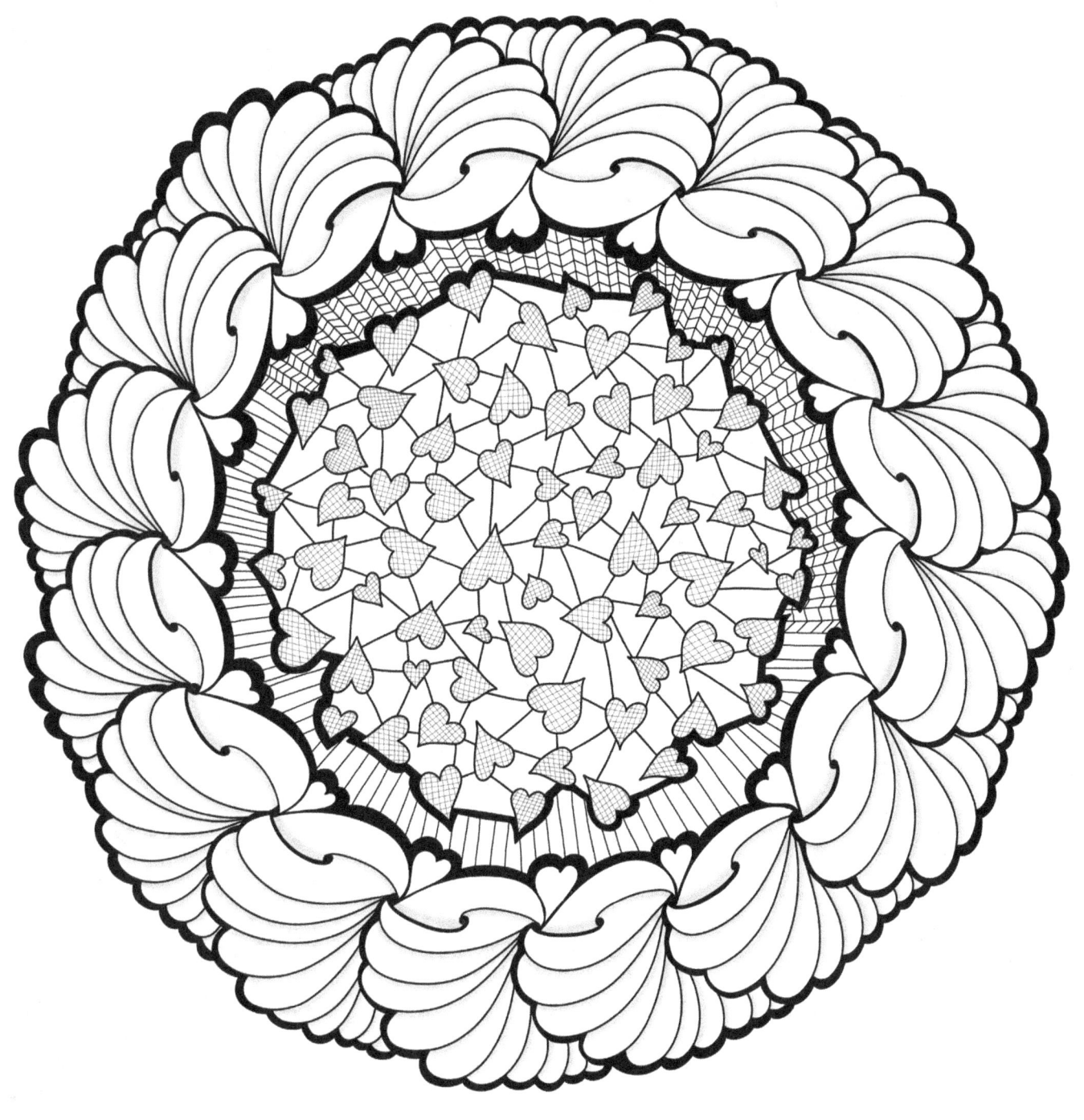

Date:_____   Colorist: _____
Media Type: _____
Media Test Area:

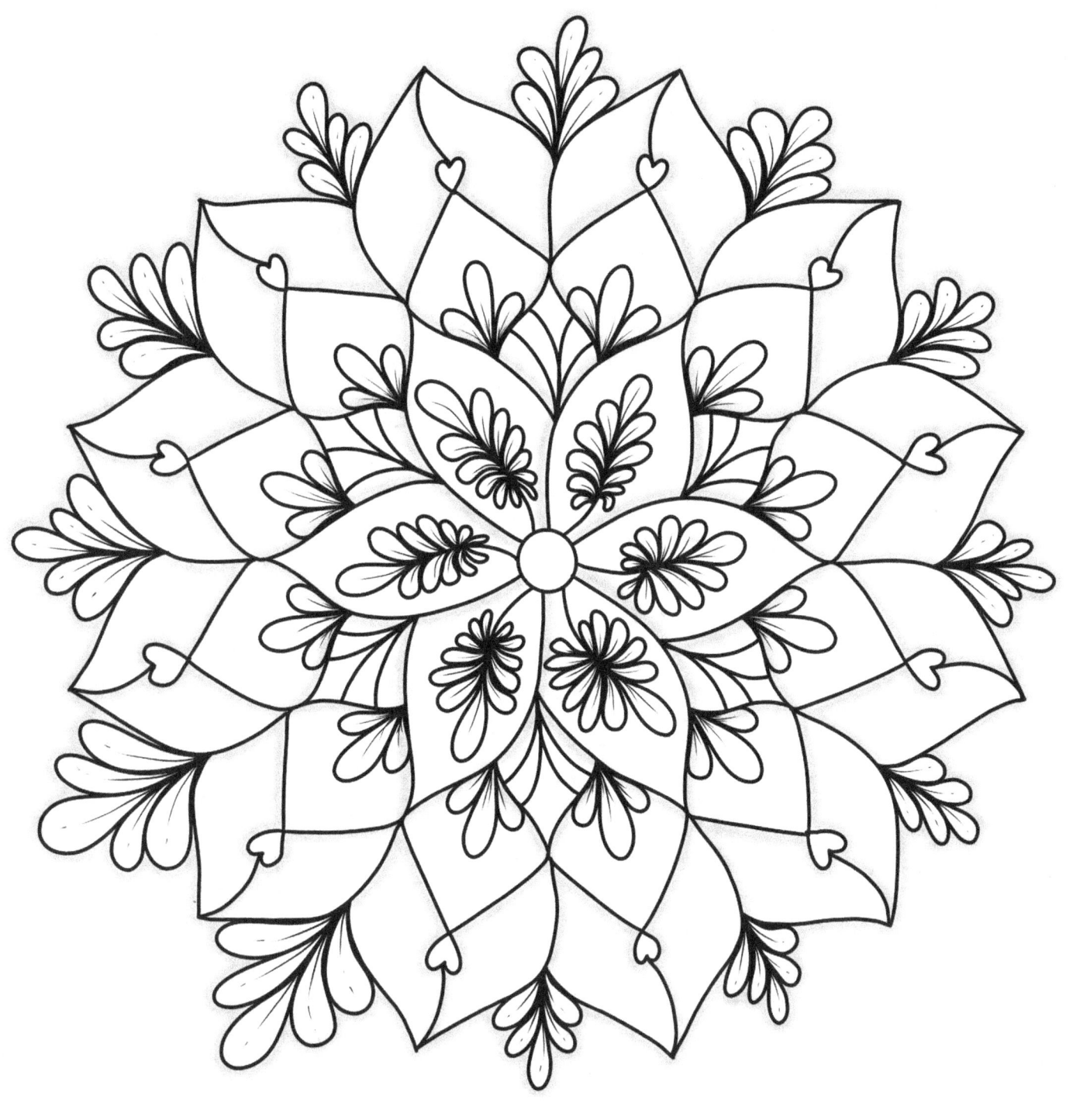

Date:_____ Colorist:_____
Media Type: _____
Media Test Area:

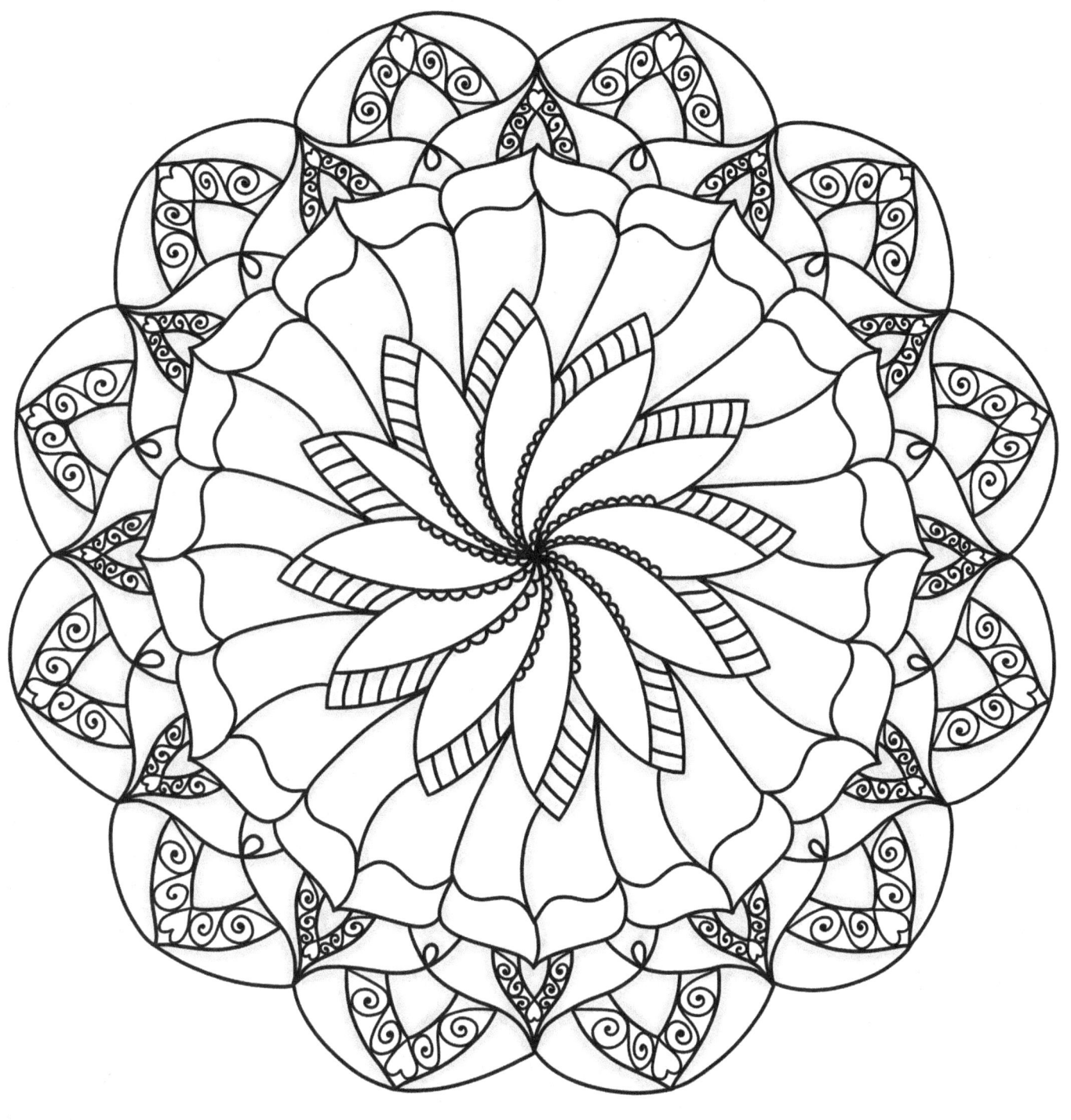

Date:_____ Colorist:_____
Media Type: _____
Media Test Area:

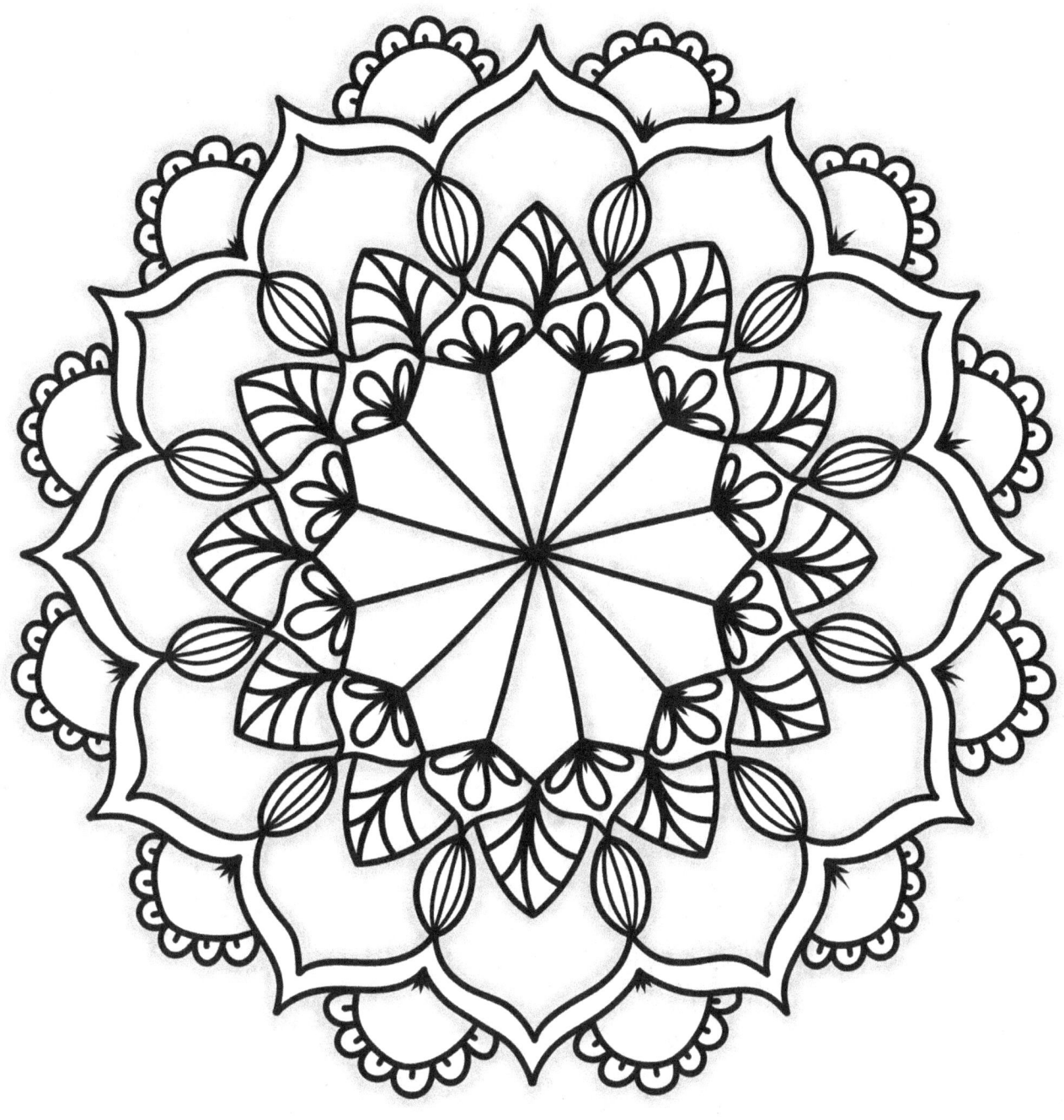

Date:_____ Colorist:_____
Media Type: _____
Media Test Area:

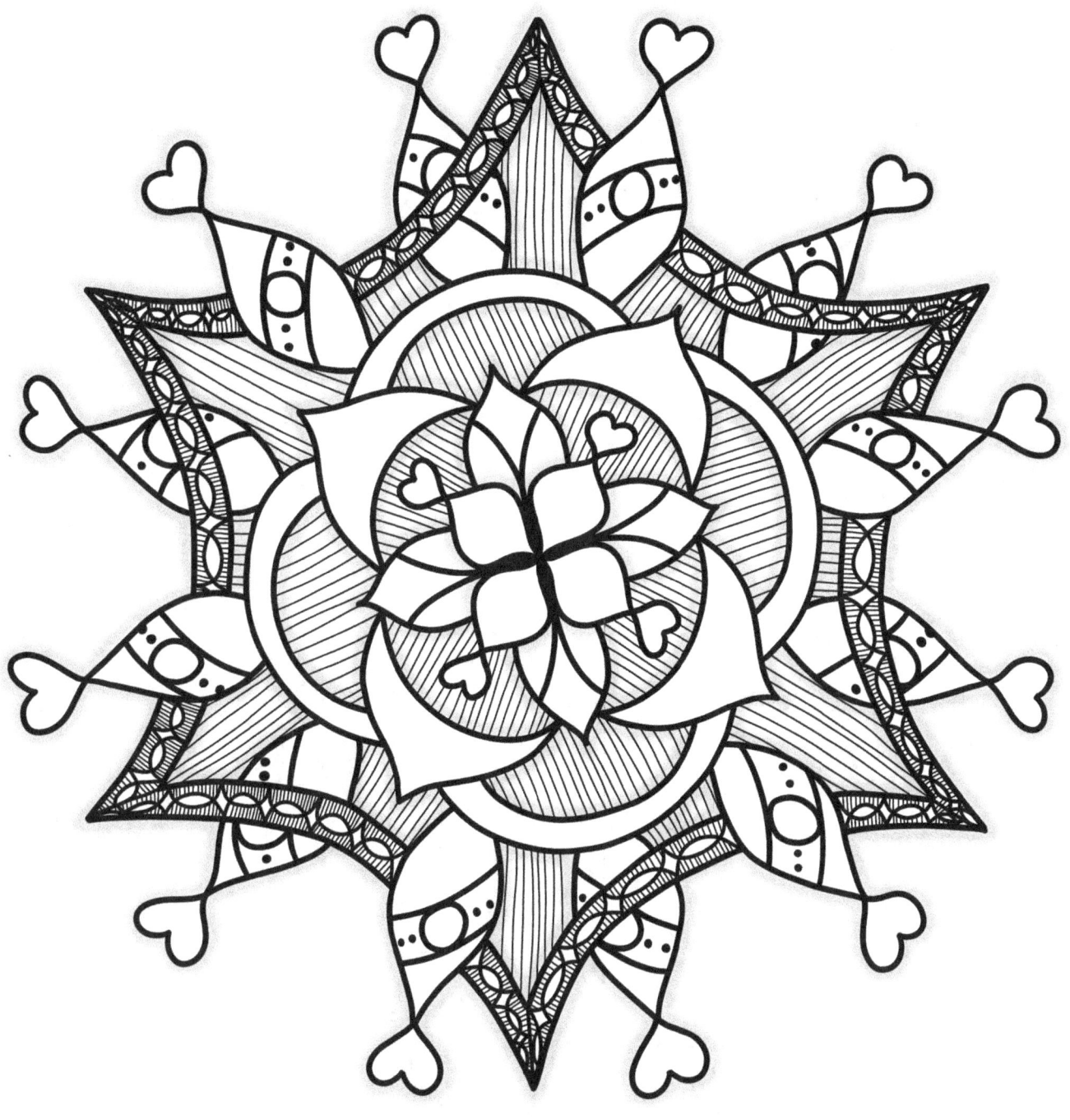

Date:_____   Colorist: _____
Media Type: _____
Media Test Area:

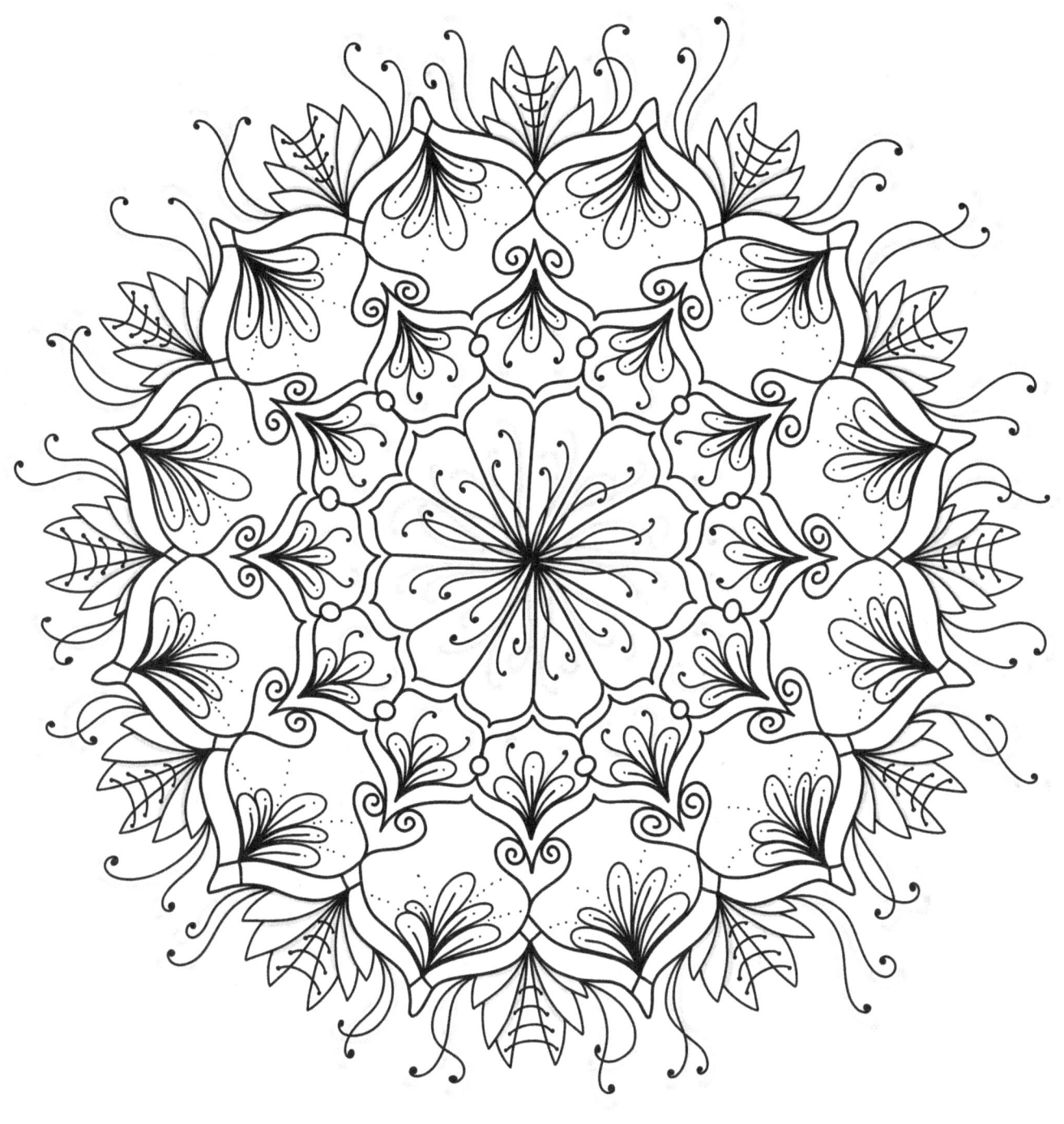

Date:_____ Colorist:_____
Media Type:_____
Media Test Area:

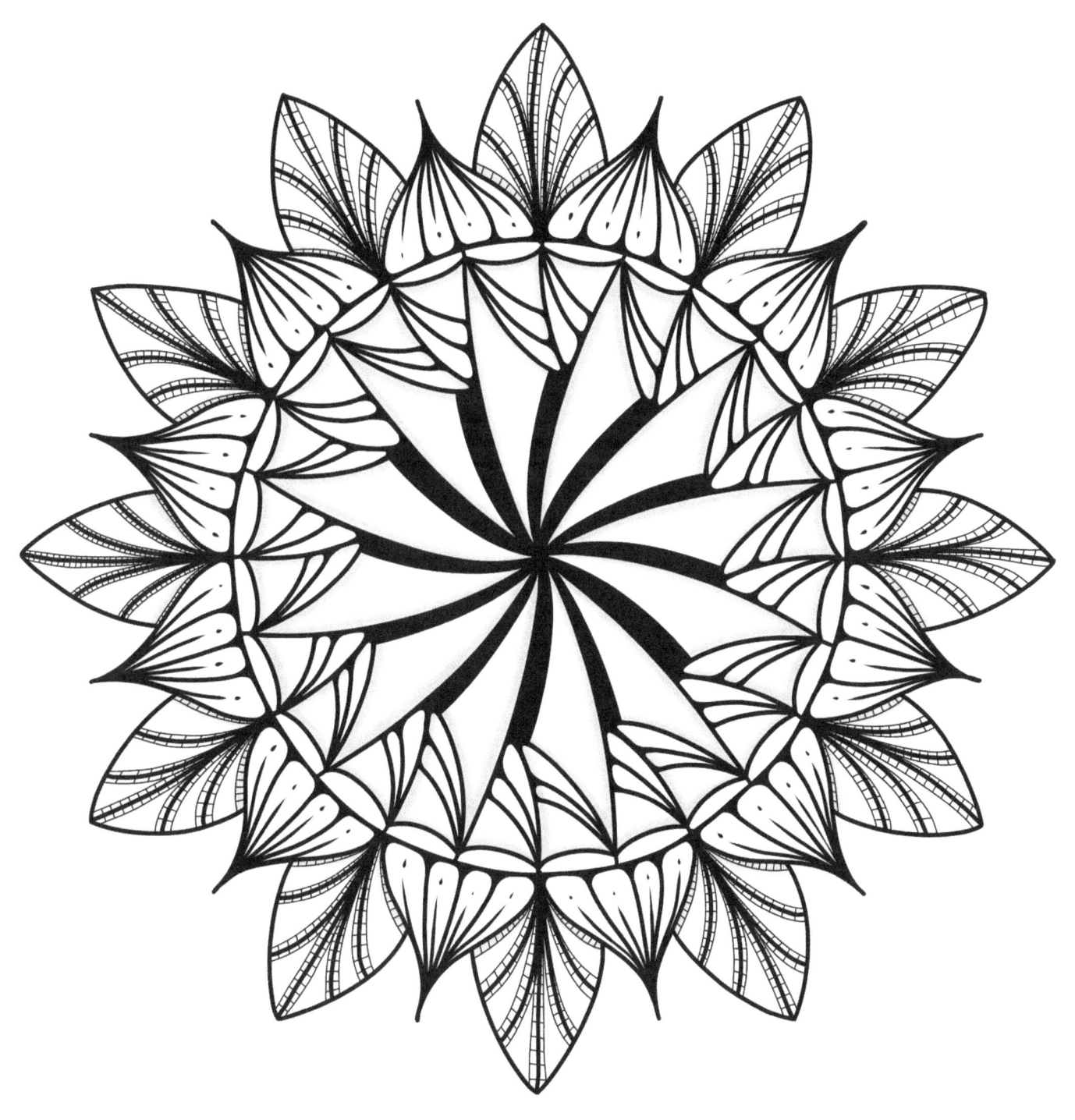

Date:_____ Colorist: _____
Media Type: _____
Media Test Area:

www.ingramcontent.com/pod-product-compliance
Lightning Source LLC
Chambersburg PA
CBHW080643240526
45466CB00034B/3155